Radically Civil

If you feel like the world has gone to hell in a handbasket, you're not alone. If you often feel there's nothing you can do about it, you're also not alone. Along with this increasing anger, fear, and frustration, much confusion still prevails on the appropriate communication practices for responding to difficult situations and improving our lives. Communication experts Robert Danisch and William Keith explain why and how we can practice radical civility in this practical guide to everyday "political" communication.

This guide begins with examples of radical civility to show the potential of this kind of communication to change minds and bridge differences. The authors then unpack the three foundational principles of radical civility as useful theoretical tools for thinking throughout interactions with others in civic spaces. This is then followed by a three-step process for practicing radical civility drawing on research into active listening and its importance for creating connections, validating other views, and opening up possibilities for future conversation. The guide concludes with evidence-based communication practices and prescriptive recommendations for how to do each and show examples of each in action.

Radically Civil: Saving Democracy One Conversation at a Time is a much-needed communication-based antidote to polarization, preparing students, researchers, and community leaders to be responsible participants in today's society.

Robert Danisch is Professor of Communication Arts at the University of Waterloo. He is the author of three monographs and a popular book on communication practices and the host of the communication skills podcast "Now We're Talking." His work has appeared in *Rhetoric Society Quarterly*, *Rhetoric Review*, *Rhetoric & Public Affairs*, *Social Epistemology*, *Public Understanding of Science*, and *Southern Communication Journal*. He teaches courses in Communication Ethics, Speech Writing, Persuasion, Small Group Communication, and Public Communication.

William Keith is Professor of Rhetoric at the University of Wisconsin–Milwaukee. He is the author of the award-winning *Democracy as Discussion: Civic Education and the American Forum Movement* and coauthor of two highly regarded textbooks, *The Essential Guide to Rhetoric* and *Public Speaking: Choices and Responsibility*. His current research focuses on the role of rhetoric and communication in public deliberation, with a focus on the intellectual and pedagogical history of the speech communication field.

Routledge Research in Political Communication

Political Leadership, Nations and Charisma
Vivian Ibrahim and Margit Wunsch

The Media, Political Participation and Empowerment
Edited by Richard Scullion, Roman Gerodimos, Daniel Jackson and Darren Lilleker

Digital World: Connectivity, Creativity and Rights
Edited by Gillian Youngs

Political Marketing
Strategic 'Campaign Culture'
Edited by Kostas Gouliamos, Antonis Theocharous, Bruce Newman, Stephan Henneberg

Politics and the Internet in Comparative Context
Views from the cloud
Edited by Paul G. Nixon, Rajash Rawal and Dan Mercea

Political Communication Online
Structures, Functions, and Challenges
Ognyan Seizov

Political Communication in the Online World
Theoretical Approaches and Research Designs
Edited by Gerhard Vowe and Philipp Henn

Discursive Disruption, Populist Communication and Democracy
The Cases of Hugo Chávez and Donald J. Trump
Elena Block

Radically Civil
Saving Democracy One Conversation at a Time
Robert Danisch and William Keith

For more information about this series, please visit: https://www.routledge.com/Routledge-Research-in-Political-Communication/book-series/PC

Radically Civil
Saving Democracy One Conversation at a Time

Robert Danisch and William Keith

Routledge
Taylor & Francis Group

NEW YORK AND LONDON

First published 2024
by Routledge
605 Third Avenue, New York, NY 10158

and by Routledge
4 Park Square, Milton Park, Abingdon, Oxon, OX14 4RN

Routledge is an imprint of the Taylor & Francis Group, an informa business

ISBN: 9781032576930 (hbk)
ISBN: 9781032580302 (pbk)
ISBN: 9781003442165 (ebk)

DOI: 10.4324/9781003442165

Typeset in Times New Roman
by Deanta Global Publishing Services, Chennai, India

Contents

Foreword

This book is for all of the frustrated, anxious, hopeless, and hopeful citizens of democracies, in the United States and around the world. That includes the students that might encounter a book like this in a college course where they can learn how to form both political and social relationships with the strangers they'll encounter as part of public and personal life. It also includes the members of civil society organizations that believe in democracy, that want to be inclusive, and that also want to see change in the world. They will find both moral and practical arguments for why we ought to be radically civil in public discourse. We hope legislators might read this too, so that they can leverage the power of communication to improve the systems they inhabit and their own connection to their constituents.

We also hope every believer of democracy, as both a system of government and a way of life, reads this, not just for political theory but for the conversational guidelines for how to live democracy as a way of life. For anyone bearing witness to the animosity, vitriol, or rancor of our public life, we intend for this book to offer hope for what democracy can still do and a recipe for how to do that work. We all find it challenging to be hopeful in our moment, given the state of polarization and the interpersonal dynamics that come with that, but locating citizenship in our everyday habits of communication (instead of in our rights) can point to a clear, constructive path forward.

Communication is the most common, mundane, and taken-for-granted activity we engage in every day; it's all too easy to take for granted how complex and difficult it is. That doesn't mean we always do it well, with style, grace, or skill. Sometimes we need a refresher on how we ought to communicate to make sure we can forge constructive, positive relationships. That's a necessary activity for citizens of large-scale democracies (and for a host of other areas of our everyday lives: navigating our workplaces, maintaining family ties, or forming new or unexpected friendships). Luckily, scholars in our field have spent the better portion of the last century identifying and explaining how communication works to form relationships and make meaning (when it works well) and how it can be destructive by generating resentment, hostility, and conflict. We intend for this book to distill some of the wisdom from scholarship in communication around the concept of radical civility. We hope readers will learn what radical civility looks like and how to practice it in communication. If all of us used these communication principles and practices, our democracy would be much healthier and our lives much less anxious and fraught. If you are able to have a radically civil conversation after reading this book, then we take that as one small, necessary step in rehabilitating our democracy. If one conversation spreads and becomes many, then our everyday interactions can become a radical resource for change.

We hope you, our readers, believe that democracy is still the best system of government and that relationships matter for our well-being. If we start from there, then this book can show you how to talk to others in the best possible ways.

Acknowledgments

We'd like to acknowledge the help and support of all the people and groups who have engaged us since the publication of *Radically Civil*, in particular, Kate Bracy and the members of Civility First in Washington State, the Braver Angels organization, and Professor David Frank, whose enthusiasm and ability to make us sound smarter than we are was endlessly inspirational.

1 The Problem and the Promise

Why Civility?

As social beings, we all deal with the same problem, every day:

How do we get along with people who are different from us?

Different tastes, different beliefs, different values, different ways to live, different ideas about the good life. These differences lead to our judgments about others, to their judgments about us, and then to clashes about how to use money, space, time, and just about everything else we can imagine. We are stuck with this, whether it's a spouse, significant other, family, neighbors, or coworkers – we are going to disagree on everything from house colors, to great movies, to the best music, to whom we can love, or how we should live.

We can resolve some of these disagreements easily – you order steak and I'll order fish, or you listen to one kind of music on your earbuds and I'll listen to another. Some are harder; the neighbor's loud music may not be to your taste or even if it is, it's just too loud. (This is not a trivial problem. Possibly half of all US residents have issues about neighbor noise. The Waycroft, 2020.) If you live with others, they may have different ideas about equitable distribution of chores or spending money on big purchases. We are deeply interconnected with others, and by living our everyday lives we end up in relationships (deep or shallow, causal, or formal) that require communicating with others. From our neighbors, to the postal carrier, to our doctor, to friends, relatives and community groups – we all have to interact with others, and our ability to just exclude people is limited. Sure, you can ghost someone (just refuse to interact with them), but not everybody. Bill Bishop and others have written about "the great sorting," which refers to people tending to move to areas where most people are politically similar to them, and they don't have to engage as much difference (Bishop, 2009). But there are always differences in what people like, believe, and do, enough to drive people nuts, it seems.

We have two systems for dealing with difference, *politeness* and *politics* (notice they share the same root, a word meaning "community"). Politeness says that you should just not comment or publicly judge other people's tastes or choices when they don't affect you directly. If they do affect you, then you

DOI: 10.4324/9781003442165-1

can ask ("politely") for a change. Politics helps us create laws, rules, and institutions to regulate things like ownership (it's not just rude to take my car, it's illegal), taxes, intellectual property, inheritance, and much more. Things do change. Smoking indoors went from polite, to rude, to illegal. On the one hand, sometimes politeness and courtesy seem to work well, while sometimes they don't get a result, and sometimes they even seem to be the problem. On the other hand, sometimes politics works well too. Actually, it works well a lot of the time, especially locally (roads are built, garbage gets collected) – but many people find it hard to understand how government works and whether or not it's working well.

These two systems seem to be on different scales, in terms of both time and space (politeness is nearby, and in the moment, while politics is far away and takes a long time). And they also seem to occupy different positions in our imaginations. Politeness seems very local and interpersonal, while politics seems distant, impersonal, and opaque. Do these two have anything in common? They are not completely different, and in fact there's a way to draw lines connecting them. We are going to use the term *civility* to identify what they have in common, both positive and negative. Since the problems solved by politeness and politics always involve multiple people, we'll define civility as a kind of relationship (among two or many people), a relationship that resides in habits, systems, and institutions. By understanding civility as a kind of relationship, we can draw politics and politeness together through an attention to communication.

What kind of relationship is a civil relationship? It involves a minimum amount of trust, willingness to listen, mutual respect, and giving the other person enough space to be different, tolerating their differences. What's the purpose of civility, of a civil relationship? When things get sticky, someone will often say "Let's keep it civil." What they mean is something like "let's keep this relationship productive and not let disagreements about our task escalate into interpersonal contempt." To help us work through differences, solve problems, and find ways to live together without violence and with manageable conflict, we turn to civility as a communicative norm focused on relationships.

Right now, civility seems broken at both the interpersonal and political level; while there was never a perfect time when everybody got along (there have always been differences), it seems that for far too many people differences have become toxic and unresolvable. One cause given for this is *polarization*, which refers to the tendency to turn small differences into big differences (often along a "liberal vs. conservative" axis), exaggerating the size and implications of the difference (McCarty, 2019). We have seen a rising tide of scholarship describing the depths of polarization and offering analyses of why we are so polarized (Klein, 2021; Mason, 2018; Mounk, 2022; Rosenfeld, 2017; Coleman, 2021). Polarization goes hand in hand with the "culture wars," where people's ordinary tastes somehow imply their radical (and polarizing) politics

(Hartman, 2019). At one point, there was considerable anger over President Obama's taste for arugula, which in retrospect seems a bit silly even though we are all caught up in this now. (Mull, 2019). We are so polarized that something that may have once just been a matter of personal preferences (Chick-fil-A or Popeye's? Rock or country music?) seems to have important political implications. It's not that there's no connection, but maybe there isn't actually a straight line from country music to authoritarianism, just a perception that reinforces itself (Kommers, 2018).

In a sense, talking about a crisis of civility is acknowledging that the personal and political spheres have come a little too much into alignment (Boatwright et al., 2019). It seems not so long ago that you could get along with people in your neighborhood and family even though you disagree about big picture political issues – we could work on good public schools and city planning, starting from divergent perspectives, without recourse to verbal and actual violence (Talbot, 2021). Most of us know that you can get along with people without agreeing about *everything*, but it seems harder now. Why? Many causes suggest themselves. The structure of social media platforms like Facebook and Instagram, with their likes/dislikes, can promote polarization on even trivial things (Beaufort, 2020). Many news outlets, apparently out of good intentions, have programs with some variation on "Red and Blue America," and even though they are trying to capture disagreement, they invite you to choose a side. Then there is what commentator Tim Miller (2022) has called "the rage juice." Sometimes it feels a lot easier and more satisfying to just pick out things from the news that will keep you enraged, and many people in different media are waiting to satisfy anyone with an addiction to the rage juice. Most people can be angry ("those damn politicians") and still be civil to their neighbors, but it can get harder and harder as the escalation of outrages seeps into daily life.

So why do we want to call our proposal radical civility? We find it radical to confront our issues with difference; we don't want to run away from the scope of our differences, or from the difficulty of resolving them. We want to embrace them. At the politeness level, we tend to solve problems by dodging them, whereas at the political level we often fight them out. Our radical suggestion is for less dodging, less fighting, and more relationship-building that leads to problem-solving. We use the word *radical* to describe civility because it gets to the root of our current broken system, marred as it is by antagonistic and resentful relationships which prevent any kind of meaningful cooperative problem-solving.

We claim that engaging respectfully with others in ways that can create meaningful connections across differences is the antidote to polarization. Those connections are essential for generating change and for maintaining the delicate social fabric that makes our lives possible. Now more than ever, we seem lost in a sea of divisive acrimony. It's as if many of us live in different worlds with different facts, different agendas, and different motivations. How do we manage to bridge those differences? This may be the most important question in our political and social lives right now. We're offering a model for how to do that work. Radical civility is a polestar to follow when dealing with difficult situations. It also gives us a communication roadmap for how best to engage all of the various characters in our lives (our racist uncle, our QAnon-believing aunt, our most difficult professional colleague, or people we perceive as our political enemies). This book will teach you how to engage others in ways that will generate systemic, non-violent change (for you and for them). Based on communication techniques which research evidence shows will work, we can explain the best methods for talking to others in these tumultuous times. And by using stories from civic organizations like Braver Angels, along with examples of intense forms of incivility, we can show how we all might move forward in building a better, more durable, and more connected democracy, while reducing the destructive forms of polarization that haunt our moment.

Let's be as clear as we can from the start: Employing practices of radical civility can reduce polarization, animosity, and resentment and allow us to have productive, problem-solving conversations. They enable a process, without determining the outcome. Too often we think about our public interactions like a zero-sum game. We think we need to win, to vanquish our opponents by scoring the most points and defending our position with the right kind of evidence and passion. But there are other options. We don't need to view our conversations in this way, as if communication were a sport that we were trying desperately to win. The vision of communication we offer in this book allows people to disagree, perhaps vehemently, but manages to show us how to create a world where people can live with differences and not give up their values and beliefs. This is the best way of making sure that differences in beliefs and values don't lead to violence, anger, hatred, and demonization of others. Radical civility allows us to make decisions and live together with those differences still in place. We need to learn how to avoid the violence and chaos that erupt when we treat our differences the way we have been recently.

The communication practices we recommend and prescribe are the necessary means for saving our democracy, pulling us back from the brink of civil war, and rebuilding an inclusive social fabric that will allow us to make good collective decisions and build durable and healthy relationships. Civility has that much promise as an ideal and a set of behaviors. It can transform encounters from angry and resentful to thoughtful and fruitful. It can be the method for generating peaceful and systemic change in our politics and to repair and improve our relationships with friends, family, and strangers. Radical civility is a strategic art, a way of getting things done when differences seem too great to overcome. Employ the principles and practices that you find in these pages and you'll have better relationships with friends and foes and maybe even create the kinds of changes you hope to make in the world. Let the polestar of radical civility orient your behaviors, and you'll be a more effective, impactful, and trusted communicator, able to form deep connections with anyone without sacrificing your own beliefs or values.

Radical civility is a new term, and on the surface, it may appear to contain a contradiction. You may already think of civility as a kind of "soft skill," the conversational lubricant necessary for making social interactions proceed smoothly (Forni, 2003). Think about all the advice columns we see online that make recommendations for how to deal with noisy neighbors, difficult in-laws, or a snarky boss (often they are "Ethics" columns"). These forms of advice allow us to avoid missteps and confusion. But we're after much more than that in this book. First, let's note that civility matters because relationships matter. This is not a trivial insight nor an end that can be accomplished with easy recommendations. Civility gives us options and habits that can reliably help us to form positive relationships with anyone. Those options and habits are increasingly important because we live in a world with ever-greater degrees of diversity. If we are asked to form relationships with people that don't look like us, sound like us, dress like us, or eat the same foods that we eat, then we can rely on the practices of radical civility to show us the way. Second, we're also social creatures. We live inside social networks, we rely on others for our well-being and support, we crave contact with friends (new and old), and sometimes we even experience the joy that can only come with the camaraderie of a team that accomplishes what one person can't (Lieberman, 2014). Our social networks live and die through specific communication practices. Use the wrong kinds of communication and your whole network of friendships and relationships can collapse. Use the right ones and it can thrive. In order to make it clear what the stakes are, we rely on the following distinction between three different kinds of civility:

> *Weak civility* These are the habits or practices of politeness, used to make other people feel comfortable in social situations. We use weak civility when we try to ignore differences. The old adage not to talk about politics or religion at the dinner table is a form of weak civility. We shy away from difficult conversations so that we can keep the peace. Etiquette manuals are manifestations of weak civility. They prescribe behaviors that reflect traditions of how people to maintain peace and order in their social lives, by respecting people and avoiding controversy. Yet the rules have a bias toward keeping the peace by avoiding politics, which doesn't help us in the current moment.

> *Weaponized civility* When we reject any talk, simply because it makes us uncomfortable, as being impolite, we are practicing weaponized civility. "How rude of you to talk about racism and mascots!" We appeal to politeness or civility to stop conversation, or silence legitimate and important disagreements. This use of civility is in bad faith and results in covering up tensions in ways that benefit some and harm others. It disengages from others and is ultimately disrespectful because of the ways

in which important disagreements are left to linger in the background. Being fake-nice often does more harm than good.

Radical civility These are behaviors and communication practices that are used to respectfully engage others in ways that deepen connections. When we listen to understand, talk about important issues to learn more, acknowledge and affirm others' beliefs and values, carefully and forthrightly share our own beliefs, and have productive and caring conversations about difficult topics, then we have engaged in radical civility. Throughout this book we will describe specific ways of enacting radical civility and offer a granular picture of radical civility in action.

We'll revisit this distinction in the different examples throughout this book. We're endorsing radical civility because of the work it is able to do, the consequences of the behaviors that make it up, and the promise it holds during these dark times of polarization and conflict.

Let's look at a few examples of this distinction at work and track some of the effects these different forms of civility are likely to produce. What does weak civility look like in action? One of us has a friend who thinks it's his job to correct other people's theology, in fairly technical ways. He's knowledgeable and means well, but it's really a bit obnoxious. The response he gets is some variation of "No kidding" or "You don't say" and then changing the subject as soon as it makes sense. That's weak civility: not confrontational, not critical, just letting it go. It's similar with any friend or relative who has wildly divergent beliefs from your own and wants to share them. What do you do? Sometimes we decide to just let it pass, with a weak version of civility, such as

How interesting
You seem fired up about that

followed by changing the subject. These responses don't trigger the person and allow you to move on without feeling conflict or discomfort. Sometimes that's the right response – but it can't *always* be the right response. Why? Because eventually it corrodes the relationship (do you really respect someone you won't even engage with?), and in a larger sense it corrodes the sense of a community of people working through disagreements on important issues. Part of what created polarization is that since we aren't engaging with each other in meaningful ways, we can develop more and more cartoonish stereotypes of each other's positions, a cycle that leads to more extreme beliefs and arguments, making it even harder to engage.

Weaponized civility is trickier. It appears when people do engage others but declare their manner or position impolite or uncivil. Fake civility is a refusal to engage based on a bad-faith appeal to civility and can take a couple of forms. Sometimes we're justified to take things off the table for civil discourse; probably there are very few people willing to engage discussions about the legitimacy of rape or murder, and that's good. But some discussions are just touchy and people are legitimately far apart. Talking about racism and sexism, in the workplace or in society at large, can be threatening for some, and they may respond that it's offensive to talk about racism or sexism. Or some people will say that their religion determines what they think about these topics and claim that it's rude to engage them. Even if these objections are offered in good faith, they are not civil. If you want to refuse to talk about something, you can say so. Not only does this approach reject engagement, but such a reaction ("That's rude") pretty directly insults the other person, further damaging the relationship. While it's likely true that there have to be some things out of bounds, strategically playing that card forecloses the maintenance of trust. Weak and weaponized civility don't require you to talk about anything uncomfortable; you can just avoid it or shift the discomfort to the other person.

Radical civility starts with the premise that a strong relationship will allow people to talk through difficult and uncomfortable topics and that maintaining that relationship will take effort and skill. One of us was thrown onto a committee with someone we didn't know, and it was going to be at least a year of working together on tough administrative issues, so relationship-building seemed important. This colleague talked all the time about guns, libertarianism, and Fox News, which was off-putting, and sometimes seemed a bit like trolling, but he came across smart and interesting otherwise. We went out for a beer. Turned out we were from the same state, had some favorite books in common, and a couple of shared hobbies. The political differences were present in our conversations, but not at the front; we just enjoyed hanging out. As the 2020 election season heated up, we had some conversations where we engaged our positions, but with a bit of openness. I was willing to allow that my favorite news outlets sometimes got things wrong, and he admitted some of the more extreme conspiracy theories weren't acceptable to him. Things got a little more heated between us after the election, and especially after January 6. It was still reasonably productive, but at one point he started a comment with "you liberals…" and I balked at that, saying "Hey don't reduce me to a stereotype," and he replied "Ok, that's fair, I know you're more complex than that." That was a great response that allowed us to continue our debate, which was making progress toward some shared understandings. Radical civility helped transform this relationship and open up possibilities that would not have been there if both people simply treated one another as enemies. We'll see examples like this, and the practices that make this interaction possible, as we move through this book.

Why Connect Communication, Politics, and Civility?

Communication, like breathing, is what we all do every day, all day long. Our communication habits shape who we are and determine how others see us.

Those habits are the most basic tools that we have for making our way through the world. We think it's important to remember that communication is not a simple matter of transmitting information from one person to another (Reddy, 1993). So much more is involved than the exchange of facts or opinions. We use communication to make meaning and to build relationships, not just acquire information. What kinds of meaning? What kinds of relationships? That all depends on how we choose to speak and write and listen and read. What we offer in this book is both more detailed than other recommendations for reducing polarization and backed by more evidence (Redmond, 2022). We are focused on the *how* of communication, in as much detail and in as practical a way as possible. Because our world is so plagued by toxic interactions, we are more in need of attention to communication than ever. We're not just referring to Instagram or Facebook or any other communication system or social media platform. Nor do we mean the "media" more generally, whatever that amorphous and ambiguous concept refers to, or forms of mass communication like movies and television. We mean the very basic ways that we choose to talk with one another, to argue with one another, and to use language to relate to one another. This is, in some ways, a call back to the basics of human communication, and that is the area of our expertise. We need now, more than ever, to collectively return to those basics. Our lives are made more stressful and anxious not from the simple fact that we happen to use new modes of communication, like Twitter or Facebook, but because our most fundamental practices of talking to one another need to be repaired and improved.

Like many people all over the world, we watched in horror as rioters attacked the US Capitol on January 6, 2021. The culmination of four years of politics that stoked divisions, anger, and hatred, that fed on tension and vitriol, and that seemed to strike at the heart of the American democratic experiment. But we have also watched uneasily while smaller acts of incivility have undermined our more local, professional, and personal lives over the past few years. We've been party to attacks on Facebook, in meetings, and by our neighbors. We imagine many of you have as well. This book offers a synthesis of all that communication can teach us to help navigate our precarious moments. Most importantly, we believe that democracy needs productive disagreement and difference. We think there's much to be gained from vigorous debate and that passion has a key role to play in bending the arc of history toward justice. At the same time, communication scholarship can best be imagined as a kind of strategic thinking, attentive to what works and what doesn't in the course of our arguments and interactions with strangers. We worry that democracies all across the globe are in decline because the social fabric that makes collective decision-making possible is being ripped apart by poor practices of disagreement and destructive ways of managing difference (Levitsky and Ziblatt, 2019). We know we need a guiding light to help us find our way out of the bitterness and resentment that seems everywhere, and we believe radical civility can act as that guiding light.

Much of what follows in this book is a critical synthesis of practical knowledge from the academic field of communication studies. Here's what we know and how it will shape what you're about to read: Too many people think of communication as a process of transmitting information from one person to another or one place to another. This is a very instrumental view of communication and it's not accurate. Many communication scholars have critiqued the limitation of what's been called the "transmission view" of communication because it unfairly reduces a complex human problem to a simple technical one (Carey, 1992; Peters, 2001). In this book, we treat communication as a complex and constitutive process (Hauser, 2002). By "constitutive" we are claiming that meaning and relationships happen in, and are created by, the communication itself. We emphasize the idea of "process" to highlight the many steps, parts, players, actions, and reactions that are part of communication. We use the word "constitutive" to claim that the complex process of communication has the power to establish, to bring into existence, or to make meaning. Meaning is intrinsic to communication. When we point at a four-legged furry creature roaming in our house and call it a "dog," we've engaged in a process of co-creating the meaning of the four-legged furry creature with the other members of our household. Since we're concerned with the human problem of communication, meaning matters more to us than information, and how we construct meaning with others poses a more difficult challenge than the technical problem of how we send information from, for example, one smartphone to another. And meaning is not in words, it is created through interacting with others (Wittgenstein, 2010). That means the practices we highlight in this book are aimed at highlighting and improving the dialogic aspects of our interactions.

If we start from the premise that communication is a process of making meaning, and that such a process is dialogic, we can begin to realize how important relationships are. This also means that argumentation, when both practiced and understood as a form of dialogue and engagement, can change minds and clarify thinking, but just being (or thinking you are) the logical and reasonable person does not. We cannot just push our logical conclusions on others; you can't be "right" before you've engaged others. Argument (exchanging ideas and reasons with others) needs to be more like ballroom dancing than boxing. We'll try to show you how, in and through the process of argument, to dance and not to box. The field of communication studies can teach us a lot about how we make relationships and how we engage in dialogic forms of argument. We'll see some of those practices later in this book. Whenever we're dancing, we need to be responsive to our partner's needs, interests, and movements. This means that we need to listen well as a first step in radical civility and a first move in argumentation. Viewed from such a perspective, communication becomes a problem-solving endeavor and not an instrumental form of manipulation. We know that manipulation doesn't work over the long run. If we force or trick someone into believing what we believe, our trickery will eventually be revealed and inevitably generate resentment (the kind of feeling that corrodes relationships). Instead of engaging in the dark arts of communication, we can find commonalities as a way of reducing polarization. If this is our starting point, what we share, then constructive relationships become possible.

Our task in the pages ahead is to show how people can collaboratively solve problems, find commonalities, build relationships, and make meaning with others. If we do all of that without falling for the temptations of communication that breeds polarization, then we can start to repair the social fabric of democracy. This is also an insight from our field that will guide this book: Democracy is a way of life and not just a system of government (Schneirov and Fernandez, 2013). As a way of life, it is associational and practiced through talking. Communication is the lifeblood of democracy, without it the system will fail (Dewey, 2016). This is also the line that connects politics to politeness. We need to learn to live well with difference in democratic societies, and that's both a problem of politics and politeness. This idea that democracy is both a way of life and a system of government is not new. John Dewey, Jane Addams, and many other American pragmatists made this argument in the late nineteenth century. Those intellectuals, philosophers, and political activists did not explicitly name civility as a democratic value, but they did name tolerance and pluralism. This book builds on the American pragmatist tradition and the desire to understand democracy as more than just the institutions of our government. Because of the ways that democracy requires collaborative and cooperative problem-solving between diverse citizens, our relationships with other citizens will always be a necessary consideration. How we manage and navigate those relationships requires more than just tolerance; we need a robust set of communication practices to live democracy as a way of life. Civility can provide that robust set of practices.

When we imagine the connection between politics, communication, and social life, we can begin to see some of the broader benefits of radical civility as well. The Harvard Study of Adult Development, which conducted the longest study on human happiness, found a strong correlation between deep relationships and well-being (Waldinger and Schultz, 2023). In other words, people that were able to forge positive, constructive relationships with others, and when those relationships endured over time and through the vicissitudes of life changes, flourished. But the study also found that we don't always put our relationships first, and we suffer because of that. The average American in 2018 spent 11 hours a day on solitary activities like watching television. Relationships affect you physically and mentally, and they take work and time and commitment. If we accept the findings of this Harvard study, then we ought to ask: How does a person develop, maintain, and nurture deep relationships? One answer is with the practice of radical civility. In other words, radical civility offers a roadmap for how one might invest in their social fitness, stave off loneliness, and reap the benefits of unexpected connections to those with different views, beliefs, and backgrounds. Viewed from such a perspective, radical civility can be both a form of civic education and personal flourishing.

This is what the critics of civility miss. Alex Zamalin and others have argued that civility is actually a tool for preserving the status quo. In *Against Civility*, Zamalin (2021) argues for what he calls "civic radicalism," and he is not alone in suggesting that material change, especially around issues of racism, cannot be achieved through civility. We have no deep quarrel with Zamalin, or any of the other scholars challenging the role that weaponized civility plays in upholding various forms of racism and sexism. But these criticisms miss the radical, foundational way that relationships can be transformative, can help us flourish, and can be the best means for opening people up to change. We share Zamalin's goals of meaningful social and political change, especially related to systemic racism, but we think those goals are more easily achieved in the presence of trusting relationships between strangers, built and maintained by practices of radical civility.

Why Now?

The time is right for a renaissance in civility. We'll leave it to the historians to decide whether our moment is unique because of unprecedented vitriol. Yet everywhere you turn you find people worrying about the future of US politics, worrying that forms of harassment, personal attacks, and open expressions of disdain are omnipresent and toxic. Some will blame the Internet, and the social media systems that have risen in popularity with it, for our circumstances. Those critiques have merit. Comments sections seem to breed vicious attacks and trolling – if we can't disagree about Star Wars without personal attacks, what chance do we stand with real disagreements? Facebook algorithms seem highly susceptible to manipulation by fake news and nasty memes, while the generalized use of attention-grabbing hyperbole in online media creates clicks that reward bad behavior with revenue (Fisher, 2022). Our speech acts online actually become valuable resources for huge companies to gather and sell data (Hari, 2022). Many books have been written about how media systems are a leading cause of our loneliness, our sadness, and our anger and outrage (Vaidhyanathan, 2021; Turkle, 2017). Many others have been written about how the Internet may be destroying democratic values (Nichols and McChesney, 2006; Taplin, 2017). Despite these troubling, dystopian assessments of our moment, the ways to make conversation better lie within our grasp.

In the early 1990s, the architects of the Internet were digital idealists and dreamers. They predicted a new dawn for democracy (Shirky, 2008; Weinberger, 2008). That new dawn has not happened. Social media may have helped make the world crazier. But partisanship, conspiracy thinking, and the politics of resentment are as old as human beings. It's true that the current design of the Internet makes it easier than ever to target, to harass, to confuse, and to lie. As we wait for systemic change, which may or may not arrive, only a renaissance in civility can stem these tides. If we are a democracy, that means we can change the rules (and certainly work needs to be done on that front). But it also means that the power of talk can redirect our current course. As we wait for new rules and policies that will help minimize the damage that social media is doing to all of us, we need the practices of radical civility to help counteract the vitriol and to help hold onto our democratic values.

A commitment to radical civility must be local, grassroots, and must start in one's own networks. This means both face-to-face encounters and our social media interactions. By using habits like active listening, we can keep our conversations going, manage our disagreements, and learn to live well with differences. That is the urgent project of the moment, because of both the ways in which technologies have rapidly reshaped our day-to-day lives and the need for our commitment to democracy to be lived in our most immediate interactions. The sudden rise in social media has coincided with the hard-won rise in diverse populations gaining access to the public square. When the French author Alexis de Tocqueville surveyed American culture in the 1830s, he saw people meeting one another, making decisions together, carrying out projects together. This was the living practice of democracy. People formed "associations" with one another everywhere. But these associations were mostly between white Western European men. Now our associations are much more diverse, thanks to the hard work of countless women and people of color fighting for the right to participate in the practice of democracy. That diversity is both a source of strength and an easy target for the vitriol, hyperbole, and anxiety of our moment. There are just many more people for us to make our "associations" with than there were when Tocqueville wrote his masterpiece on democracy. So, we have more people to get along with and these communication systems that seem to lend themselves to the kinds of talk that destroy democratic values. This is our predicament. And that predicament calls us back to the basic forms of human communication that can build and sustain constructive relationships between strangers.

We've learned a lot about networks in recent years. We've learned about the importance of strong ties and weak ties, how companies like Google and Pixar create innovative teams of people with diverse skills, and about how our social networks can lead to confirmation bias and blind us to new evidence and ideas (Pentland, 2015; Catmull and Wallace, 2014; Granovetter, 1973). All of those insights are wonderful and important. But what are the practices by which we can sustain our networks? Mediated or face to face? If we don't answer that question, then all that we know about networks may not help us revive our dying democracy. That's why we need a sustained consideration of civility now more than ever. People are problems-solvers, at least people that live democratic values are. This is what Tocqueville saw in his journey. The best way to solve problems is through discussion. If we are to solve our problems through discussion, we need to know how good communication (and argument) can manage disagreement and facilitate change. Or how bad communication can allow disagreement to devolve into violence and how it might stop change in its tracks. A commitment to civility teaches us that rightness and wrongness are less important than how we treat others. That's because we are all fallible, and what's right today may appear wrong tomorrow. Relationships are more likely to endure than opinions about rightness and wrongness. As soon as we recognize that, we can begin the journey of building our civility skills.

After you read this book, you'll know what to write on a Facebook post so that you might have a productive conversation with a long lost relative or friend. You'll also know what to say to your colleague who voted for someone you loathe or who constantly reminds you of where they keep their guns for the coming apocalypse. You'll even know what to tell your grandfather who is questioning the safety of the latest vaccine. Beyond that, you'll know how to engage in difficult political conversations about the most pressing issues we face: climate change, voting rights, racism, and economic inequality. And you'll know how to do that work regardless of the side of these issues that you currently find yourself on. You'll also know how to respond to someone that appears flooded with extreme emotions and rage, regardless of the source of the rage. You'll find yourself able to build relationships with strangers and enter into meaningful conversations that you never would have predicted. These basic, foundational communication skills are what we all need right now to talk to anyone about anything. They'll give us the confidence to navigate our lives strategically and effectively, without the fear and anxiety that seems ever-present.

We also need to recognize how badly trust in our public institutions has eroded in the last few years. Institutions of government and civil society have long been central instruments in maintaining the social order. We can't simply blame new media for sowing distrust; we also have to recognize that those institutions no longer function as they once did to create the social glue that might hold us all together. This is why we need radical civility now more than ever: If we distrust our institutions, then a relational approach to managing difference is all that we have to do the necessary trust-building work. A relational approach to communication, practiced by both citizens and civil servants, is one of the few resources that could potentially build back a quotient of trust to help preserve the social order. Knowing what to say, and how to say it, to strangers or citizens with deeply different beliefs is the best, and perhaps only, resource we have for trust-building when we are suspicious of all the institutions that surround us (the media, local government, school boards, regulatory agencies, etc.). This is another way of saying that democracy needs a functional social system. We need civility now more than ever to maintain that social system.

Why Be Civil When Others Are Not?

One of the deepest, and at the same time one of the simplest, challenges of democracy happens when our fellow citizens treat us – and others – with bad faith, refusing to commit to constructive conversation. We see this when racists demean whole groups of citizens with derogatory names and other harmful speech acts. Why, then, be civil to a racist when that person would never be civil toward you? Let's first look at why this is a situation where civility, generally a good thing, seems wrong and then examine the reasons for mostly sticking with civility.

Two situations of asymmetric civility present themselves. First, there is morally unacceptable, and therefore uncivil, behavior (like casually using a racial slur) and second, deliberately nasty behavior. Let's consider each in turn. The intuition that some actions, language, and beliefs are beyond the realm of civil social relations is understandable and reasonable. Civility, in general, is a commitment to equality, and treating others (even if they aren't present) with contempt or disrespect doesn't enact that commitment. Often the person will say "I don't mean any harm" or "I was just joking," but that doesn't exactly solve the problem, and we still have to decide how to respond. In this case, there are civil ways of indicating your discomfort and challenging the behavior; you can always say "Wow, actually I'm really uncomfortable with that word, can you use a different one?" Sometimes the person will agree and take up your suggestion. Sometimes they will just say "I don't agree" or "Too bad," and go on as before. This response edges up to the second problem, the deliberately nasty, uncivil, or offensive person. This person may not care about the effect on you or may actively enjoy seeing you squirm.

Both cases present a choice, a practical and ethical choice: Should you respond to their bad behavior with some incivility or nastiness of your own? Hit back, on your own or someone else's behalf? Should you engage the person in a (civil) discussion of what you have a problem with, or shun them and encourage others to shun them as well? In a way, this is analogous to other kinds of bad treatment. If someone steals from you, should you steal from them? If someone insults you, should you insult them back? If someone shows anger toward you, is it necessary to be angry in return? If someone hits you, should you hit them back if you don't need to?

One reason is to think that we would value relationships enough to search for ways to not totally break them over disagreements about what's offensive or disrespectful. Our understanding of equity and respect is complex and continually evolving, and we should admit, with some humility, that we are probably as imperfect at times as this person. Polarization is what results when we push people away for mistakes or being mistaken. There's no question that sometimes cutting someone off can be the right thing to do, either because you have no real reason to interact with them again or because you've put in some work and things aren't changing. But the perspective of radical civility values persuasion – the attempt to gently change other people's minds through argument and example. Why should you be civil to a racist? Because you might be able to change their mind, and because in most cases they are much more than a racist – a friend, a brother, a valued coworker with other redeeming qualities that make it worth the work.

Another reason people resist being civil to people who espouse reprehensible views is that they fear by even tolerating the person, let alone engaging them civilly, they are somehow approving their views, or that not shunning the person becomes, by extension, a kind of racism or sexism. These are valid worries, and in specific cases, it can be right to act on them. Yet we need to recognize that we are all flawed, all make mistakes, all hold views that others find offensive. Universalizing this logic would make it all but impossible to have robust relationships except in small groups of like-minded people. Perhaps that seems like an exaggeration, but the evidence on polarization in the early twenty-first century suggests that many people do find it difficult to form and maintain relationships that reflect the political diversity of their communities. Of course, we meet others who offend our values, who we believe are contributing to the world being a worse place for others – or are they? A thoughtful conversation might help you understand just how "bad" their beliefs are: Was it just a thoughtless word choice? A shallow stereotype that cropped up? Or a deep belief that they act on in ways that harm others? Do you object to the totality of their values, or just a specific point? Probably the Golden Rule is appropriate here. In most cases, you'd like someone to have a conversation with you before judging you, and it's fair that in all but the most extreme cases you would give someone else the same chance.

What to Expect

This is not (just) a book about personal improvement. You may learn useful tools that will help you become a better person, but we are after a bigger goal. We want to show how you can transform the public setting in which you communicate. We speak worlds into existence by how we choose to speak – can you choose, and enact, a better world than this one? Those public settings may be professional, civic, or social, but you need to be able to build strong, durable relationships with anyone. Here's the picture we want to work with:

Build civil relationships →
    Work to understand each other→
        Argue about issues from within relationships of understanding→
            Make choices together as cities, states and country

We're trying to escape superficially good relations – what people sometimes mock as "kumbaya" – and we don't assume everybody will eventually get along and agree. (If that were possible, we'd work on that instead of civility.) A democracy needs people to have clashes of opinion and argument. It needs a civility which allows people to disagree. Radical civility, as the guardian of the process, is the goal of dialogue, not consensus or a specific kind of agreement. We're not trying to convince you to become a liberal or a progressive or a conservative. We want to show you a way to create a world in which people can live with their differences and not give up their values and beliefs. A world where arguments do not have to produce one winner and one loser. Such a world would include less violence, anger, and hatred for those with whom we disagree. We want to show you how to reconstruct civil society around basic communication practices so that we have better relationships of all kinds. And how we can argue without the need to win at all costs.

That's a tall order, and in the rest of the book, we will take the promise and add to it *Principles* and *Practices* to get to the *Payoff*. Let's start with a discussion of the three core principles of strong civility.

1. Connect first
2. Keep complexity in mind
3. Sit with productive discomfort

The first principle is that we need to try to connect with people before we try to convince them or persuade them of our position. When we have worked to bond with people, finding commonalities and connections with them, we can have (some) trust. And when there is trust, it's easier to disagree, to try on new and uncomfortable positions, to consider arguments and evidence we normally reject. In the end, we still may reject them. But in the process, change is possible. What creates a brick wall? Too often, we think that if we just marshal the right arguments or bombard people with enough facts that they will bend to our will. These are called "push tactics" of persuasion; they almost never work, since no one likes to be bullied or manipulated, they leave people feeling defensive and less willing to engage you. Instead, we ought to give up our desire to start by proving we're right and replace it with attempts to form authentic connections. We can only be successful at persuasion if we have a durable bond with someone else.

The second principle is to treat other people as multi-dimensional and complex and to acknowledge that people can and do change. Our habits are often reducing people to a specific belief or two, as if knowing someone was a Republican or Democrat, watches Fox News or listens to NPR, likes Taylor Swift or Toby Keith told you everything you needed to know. One-dimensional stereotypes prevent us from forming strong bonds with others; once you start thinking in terms of good guys and bad guys, there isn't going to be room for real engagement. All of us hold a wide variety of opinions, beliefs, values, and philosophies, some of which may be contradictory. That's okay, and actually may be an advantage. Once we start seeing the complexity of people, we can more confidently treat them with civility.

The third principle is to lean into hard conversations and practice self-discipline in these conversations, especially when we are uncomfortable. Not running away is hard! This skill is critical to radical civility because we need to recognize that we're not just being nice. These hard conversations are where respect is earned, where we come to really understand others, and where people can feel their dignity is affirmed. To have such conversations, we need to keep our own emotions in check. We'll explain why each of these principles matter, how we can enact them, and why they work.

Once we've got the principles down, we describe the dimensions of civil conversations, and the most important part of that is active listening. We begin conversation there because listening is what allows us to generate understanding and show people that they've been heard. Active listening orients the project of radical civility, so we show you how to do it and why. Next, we discuss how to keep conversations going. We are particularly concerned with moving people from emotionally reactive and charged states to more careful and sober kinds of interactions. With the right techniques, conversations can be generative and move in interesting directions, instead of suddenly ending with animosity and resentment. Finally, we describe deliberation, which is the process of making choices together. Strong civility, when enacted in the ways we describe, will ultimately lead to deliberative conversations. These conversations produce good decisions and make people feel fulfilled, optimistic, and connected to a well-functioning community. Attend to the dimensions of radical civility and your conversations will be more meaningful and rewarding.

In the fourth part of this book, we get into the details, the do's and don'ts of communication in any situation. We've made a list of ways of talking to embrace and what to avoid. This list works wherever you are in the process of conversation and whoever your audience is. The list includes examples and counterexamples, and some scripts for what to say and how to say it. This list also represents some of the most foundational and basic forms of human communication that we know work well. These practices are really the lifeblood of radical civility and the means by which we can lean into hard conversations without seeing them devolve into destructive fights. Once we've gone through our list of what to do and what to avoid, then we describe the payoffs for radical civility. You'll see that even in the hardest cases, we can still create change and use the principles and practices of radical civility to build bonds with people. At the end, you'll find the argument that what we've outlined is the best way for us to save the democratic experiment and rebuild our social fabric. Let's get started by first describing the principles that ought to guide our communication practices and our conversations.

2 The Principles

Principles of communication are not grand philosophical statements that attempt to identify a-cultural or trans-historical truths. We are not proposing something similar to Immanuel Kant's categorical imperative. These principles are meant as guidelines, or rules of thumb, that can be adapted and applied in many circumstances in order to produce positive outcomes. They are also ways of synthesizing existing scholarship in communication and rhetoric so that we can arrive at some practical recommendations for enacting radical civility in the various politically charged circumstances that we might find ourselves in. Broadly sticking to these three principles gives us the best chance to form meaningful and constructive relationships with those that differ from us.

Principle #1 – Connect Before You Try to Convince or Persuade

When we think about differences of opinion, belief, and policy, how do we approach them? Do we tolerate those differences, let them be, or do we try to change the other person? A spate of recent books and articles about persuasion display a desire to strategically overcome people's stubborn resistance to reasoned argument (Bowden, 2022; Hayward, 2018; Williams, 2020; Clark, 2022). Take, for example, Eleanor Gordon Smith's (2019) *Stop Being Reasonable*, a book in which the author goes out to the city streets to convince men to stop catcalling women. Smith, a philosopher by training, believes that if she just presents enough evidence to these men, she'll be able to get them to change their behavior. Of course, it doesn't work, despite all the reason-giving, men can seemingly rationalize catcalling under any circumstances. Or we might consider Robert Cialdini's best-selling books *Pre-Suasion* (2018) and *Influence* (2006), which help explain how automatic physiological responses to specific forms of communication are key because manipulating these automatic responses improves the chances of getting the results we want from any given interaction. Notice the asymmetry, though – when we disagree with someone, we naturally start by thinking the problem is that *they* are different, not us. The question that both authors address is something like this: "How

DOI: 10.4324/9781003442165-2

can *we* (the smart, reasonable, well-informed, and righteous ones) convince *them* (the uninformed, bigoted, uneducated, or backward) to believe or do the right thing?" Yet an obsession with persuasion, because we see it as the key to getting what we want, to winning, or to bending the world to our will or view, has serious limitations (not least of which is how infrequently it works!). This one-way stance seems to be the general outlook of the members of the United States Congress, where few people engage each other in a way that suggests they seek a middle ground. We might call this an *instrumental* view of both communication and democracy, where the purpose of both is to advance your own cause as effectively as possible. Even though it's common sense to many people, and useful in some situations, we want to provide an alternative, one we think is more effective.

The assumption of the instrumental perspective is that the goal of any disagreement is to end the disagreement in our favor – to "win" (Goldstein, 2009). Yet this isn't compatible with the practice of radical civility. If you've ever found yourself the target of a persuasion attempt, you probably noticed you were digging your heels in, maybe a bit unreasonably – somebody was pushing, so you pushed back, harder. You experienced the significant short-coming of the instrumental approach; it asks you to respond in kind. You dig in because you sense that you are playing a power game, in which the person trying to persuade you is demanding that you act in an open-minded way while remaining closed-minded themselves. We call these forms of persua-sion, like the instrumental use of argument, *push* tactics of communication. In addition, we call the psychological tricks Cialdini describes "compliance" tactics. These push/compliance tactics of persuasion are now unfortunately how most people think about communication; people think these are "realis-tic" pathways and we have almost forgotten there are other options. Yet let's think about what happens when you are literally pushed: We either stumble backward or stiffen up to absorb the force. In any case, when we are pushed, our fight or flight instincts are engaged and we get ready to go to battle or we withdraw. These are not good outcomes in any communication process. "Compliance" seems negative; it implies a lack of agency or control, since we are forced to comply. "Push" tactics of persuasion generally don't work very well. They're more likely to alienate people, create divisions, and strengthen people's existing beliefs (the beliefs we are trying to change). Compliance tactics work in the short run to secure a particular outcome, but they rarely produce durable changes. This is what Eleanor Gordon Smith found out when she tried to persuade men to stop catcalling – they just become more con-vinced that what they were doing was just fine. These push tactics of persua-sion run up against the psychological phenomenon called "reactance" (Brehm and Brehm, 1991). Whenever we feel that our agency is being taken away from us, we resist whatever we see as the source of that threat to our agency, even if it means that we adhere more strongly to a belief that might be false or that might hurt us. Reactance is a powerful drug that leads people to hold problematic and destructive positions, but every time we push someone to change their beliefs or behaviors to align with ours, we set off this feeling of reactance.

Disagreements, arguments, or conversations (whatever word you prefer) ought to be more than just opportunities to force people to align with your own specific and insular view of the world. What's the alternative? If you're only focused on instrumental persuasion, then you'll never deeply hear the other person (and as we'll see in the next section, that's a key step in the process of practicing radical civility). It can be hard, and sometimes scary to think about another model of dealing with difference, because it seems risky. What if we change? We sometimes don't listen because we close off, from the get-go, the possibility that we might change our own views. In *Finite and Infinite Games*, James Carse (1987) distinguishes between games that are played for the purpose of winning (finite games) and the game – there is only one, and its human social life – that is played for the purpose of continuing to play (infinite games). Chess, football, basketball, these are finite games; they end when one side wins and the other loses, and they are zero sum, since somebody has to win and somebody has to lose. We often look at the big, public questions of policy and value like that and end up frustrated.

What if we understand democracy as an ongoing way of life and not just a system of government that can be gamed to win? Maybe democracy is an infinite game. This means that democracy has no end outside itself; we do it together because doing it is ethical and makes our lives better. Players may win or lose in the course of play (Democrats or Republicans may achieve a legislative victory by passing a law that enshrines their priorities), but those wins and losses are just moments in an unfolding process. In a finite game, the rules exist so that the game can come to an end, and a winner and loser can be declared. In an infinite game, like democracy, the rules are framed around ways to extend the game, to keep the conversation going (another key part of the process of radical civility described below), and not providing "moves" that allow "sides" to win or lose. Of course, people may form coalitions and temporarily see themselves as a side which wants to win, but that is self-defeating if it's the only stance you take, or if it causes the game to collapse. The same is true in the non-political arenas of human collaboration. Marriages and business enterprises go well when participants see disagreements as part of an ongoing process and not simply as a locally instrumental, win–lose affair. The aim of an argument between married partners ought to be to challenge the relationship to make it stronger, just as the aim of a workplace argument is to secure a better future for the organization. But sometimes we want to win so badly that we mistake local wins for global success. This is what is plaguing our democracy in our current moment; winning by destroying the game isn't really winning.

If we think about democracy as a way of life, then it becomes important to think about how we connect with strangers in order to make decisions. In this model of democracy, relationships matter because they endure (beyond just a single-issue debate), and conversations are oriented around problem-solving not winning or losing; maintaining the relationship is more important than changing the other person in the moment. The first principle of this book is that we ought to seek to connect with others before we seek to persuade them. Radical civility asks that we drop the instrumental focus on persuasion and replace it with a focus on using communication to build relationships.

We might think of this as prioritizing relationality over persuasion. *Relationality* is admittedly an odd word. We use it here to highlight the ways in which a commitment to radical civility asks that we put relationships ahead of persuasion in the communication process. In our interactions with others, we act with radical civility when we are engaged, open, and respectful of others in hopes of establishing or maintaining a meaningful relationship. A relational way of communicating involves taking an open, positive attitude into our interactions with everyone, assuming that they are acting out of good motives (or, at least, not assuming they're acting out of malice) – and also that their failures might just be attributable to something that we could understand and relate to if we knew them as a friend. This holds for people we know well and those who are total strangers to us. Additionally, living in a relational way calls us to interact with others in a manner that lets them know that we are going to treat them as we would treat a true friend – even in situations involving conflict, and even when they act in ways that threaten us, frighten us, or trigger our reactivity. It means not responding with violence or using power to intimidate and control another person.

To prioritize relationality, we need to foster, and engage in, quality dialogue instead of instrumental persuasion. We use the word *dialogue* here to draw attention to the ways we can open up conversations or discussions. Quality dialogue requires many of the communication practices we identify later in this book. For now, we can contrast relationality with a transactional approach to communication. Transactional communicators want to know what they are going to get out of a relationship; they "use" others and act from self-interest. When choosing how to act in situations where we might not see or talk to another person again, we tend to communicate in whatever way maximizes our self-interest, as if the relationship with that other person is of no value and not a consideration. We act like economists, constantly calculating return on investment in every relationship. Classic examples of a transactional stances include a student cheating off another student's paper in school; a driver cutting in front of someone in traffic or running a red light; a shopper buying something, taking it home, using it, and then returning it and asking for a full refund; the restaurant patron demanding great service and leaving no tip; a customer ignoring and never even making eye contact with a cashier. These acts erode our sense of community ("Am I going to be exploited next?"). In contrast, relationality approaches communication as more than our needs and desires and prioritizes the quality of our relationship with another person as the core of our own self-interest. The Jewish theologian Martin Buber (1971) made a useful distinction between "I–it" relationships and "I–thou" relation-ships. In an "I–it" relationship, the other person is an object for our use and persuasion is the way we use that person. An "I–thou" relationship requires meeting a person where they are, respecting them as a person just like us, and connecting with them on an authentic level.

We might mistake the fearless pursuit of self-interest for leadership in our political culture because such people can often be direct, willful, uncompro-mising, and effective at achieving certain results in the short run. Some people are very good at navigating "I–it" relationships. But this is not genuine leader-ship because those transactional and self-interested people are not capable of building durable and lasting bonds with others. Leadership requires a degree of authentic interest in the well-being of others alongside an openness to dia-logue and conversation characterized by a pursuit of mutual understanding. These are qualities of communication that we can forget if we focus too much on transactional goals or the transmission of information. These qualities of communication are also necessary for producing trust, and trust works as a kind of precursor to the process of persuasion.

The mantra we ought to follow is "connect before you try to convince," and by this we mean that relationality should be a priority if you hope to persuade someone, because they will listen differently to you if you have a strong, connected relationship. This might be as simple as checking in with others' feelings or concerns. In business settings, it might mean devoting more time to trying to understand employees' lives, goals, hopes, values, and concerns before making decisions or pursuing agenda items. For example, at one of our first department meetings with a new Chair, the department spent the first 20 minutes of the meeting going around the room, each saying some-thing about what we were working on that we really cared about that semester. At first, this didn't seem like a good use of time, but when people saw how genuinely interested the Department Chair was and how good everyone felt sharing their thoughts and goals, the value of connection became clearer. The mood in the room changed, people felt differently connected to one another, and this action set the tone for much of the rest of the year for the department.

Focusing on connection instead of persuasion actually improves our chances of creating durable and meaningful change, and without these con-nections we diminish our chances of creating change. Evidence across a range of scholarly fields confirms this. Think about the ways our social networks can help us lose weight or stop smoking (Christakis and Fowler, 2011). Here, social ties are the key to behavior change. Think about the ways new relation-ships can help us think differently; how a dynamic teacher makes us feel seen or heard and in so doing alter the course of our lives. When we trust people, when we feel close to them, we are less likely to dig in to defend our beliefs and more likely to open ourselves up to different insights or evidence. The process of influence also becomes a two-way street whereby we impact our trusted conversational partner and our connection to this other person can change us both in unexpected ways. The benefit of connecting before trying to convince is that the rapport we establish with another person defuses defensiveness, breaks the cycle of instrumental communication, establishes a relationship built on trust, and opens up the possibility of genuine, collaborative problem-solving. These are the circumstances when real change can happen, and without connections (or strong relationships) we diminish our chances of creating change.

A former Director of family planning for Chelan-Douglas County, Washington, told us a story that shows the value of connecting before trying to convince. The clinic that she worked for was broken into, offices sabotaged, and doctors threatened; one letter to the editor of a local newspaper compared her to a Nazi. Instead of pushing back against the letter writers and those attacking their offices, this person decided to patiently wait for an opportunity to find common ground with the local opponents of abortion. She recognized the complexity of the issue and sought an opportunity to connect with the leaders of anti-abortion groups in her area. She decided to ask for an initial meeting with two local Catholic Priests, two Mormon Elders, the head of a local organization called Birthright, a local head of the National Organization for Women, the leader of a local Right to Life chapter, and a local leader of the American Association of University Women. During the first meeting, the Catholic priests sat with their backs to the rest of the group. Instead of defending Family Planning with this group or trying to push a set of arguments on an unwilling group of priests and activists, the meetings tried to generate some kind of connection out of all of these differences. Within 3 months, the group had found common ground and formed a non-profit organization devoted to support for teenage mothers that had decided to keep their babies. After this breakthrough, the Family Planning center could feel the de-escalation of tension and the break-ins stopped. According to the Director of family planning: "This is the only time in my life I ever felt I had political power." That power came from the coalition of those on opposing sides around a common ground that they discovered by their willingness to connect before trying to convince. The state legislators that they spoke with gave them money for their work almost immediately because they simply didn't know what to do with a group composed of people that were so often fighting.

How do you connect before you try to convince? First, avoid *compliance* and *push* tactics of persuasion. If you start by thinking "I can get this person to agree with me," you are doomed. This means we should drop the emphasis on the tools of reciprocity, social proof, and the other psychological tricks. If these tactics are more prevalent than the practices of radical civility, then we're in trouble, because developing civil relationships will be almost impossible. We need to stop trying to beat opponents into submission by shoving evidence at them in hopes that they will relent and admit defeat. Academics often do this in their own disciplines, but it's not the way to communicate as democratic citizens. Instead, we can follow the advice of Marshall Ganz (2009), who has spent his career following the advice of Saul Alinsky (1989) (who, despite his reputation, advocated a kind of radical civility). These two figures are central proponents of social movement building as a way of creating change. When Ganz trained volunteers for Barack Obama's first campaign for the presidency, he taught them to share with strangers their personal story (Danisch, 2012). He called this the "story of self," a bit of authentic self-disclosure. He taught his volunteers to elicit a "story of self" from whatever stranger they were talking to. They did this instead of talking about policies, or even about the candidate. The purpose of these personal acts of self-disclosure was to create the possibility for connection. If two people were then able to see themselves as part of a larger "story of us," then that's what built a movement capable of electing a president or changing the political course of the country. Ganz learned these practices from Alinsky, who spent much of his time in "house meetings" talking with all sorts of people about their experiences and concerns before attempting any direct political action. During these house meetings, a social movement organizer like Alinsky would attempt to meet people where they were, to speak their language directly, and to relate to people in authentic ways.

When we tell our story, or listen to someone else's personal story, we can connect our experience to theirs, which helps us identify values that we share, instead of focusing on facts that divide us. We connect over values more easily than we do over facts or abstract theories. These stories *show* rather than *tell* our values and perspective. We don't have to come out and declare that we believe in free speech or abortion rights; we tell a story which shows what values have oriented our decisions in life, providing grounds for connection instead of the grounds for arguing to convince. Stories are a "pull" tactic of persuasion in that they try to bring us closer to whomever we are talking with. We can think generally about connection as the kind of communication that can pull us closer to others. Ganz and Alinsky knew that whatever policy issue was causing controversy one day would be replaced by a new issue, which means my ally would inevitably at some point be on the other side. But if I shared enough with the people in my community, and if I was connected to those people in meaningful ways, then the bonds of connection would sustain our relationship through any temporary agreement or disagreement on a controversial issue. Simply put, our relationships matter more than winning the day on some issue; note that "winning" doesn't mean you don't advocate for a side of an issue, it just means that you can't win if you make an ally into an enemy. These organizers also knew to test the strength of a connection before venturing into territory that might be controversial or contentious. Alinsky often did this with self-deprecating humor, gently teasing people to find out the strength of his connection to others; if we can laugh together, we can get things done. We all should test our connections before attempting any form of instrumental persuasion or advocacy. This would prevent much of the misunderstanding and acrimony that seems so ever-present right now.

Stories aren't the only method of connecting with others before trying to convince them. We can often do more through asking questions than by telling others what to do. Good questions can help build positive relationships in ways that telling cannot. This is because good questions show a recognition that others might have valuable knowledge that we would benefit from, and when we show others this kind of interest, we are able to build relationships based on mutual respect. Not all questions, however, are equal. The kind of questions that we think are most valuable can be described by the phrase "humble inquiry," the kinds of questions that draw someone into a conversation (Schein, 2013). One characteristic of such questions is that the person asking does not already know (or think they know) the answer. Beginning from genuine doubt will allow the relationship to evolve from curiosity and interest in the other person. To develop good relationships and reliable, honest communication between and across hierarchical boundaries, we often need to ask the kinds of questions that manifest our interest in others. Building relationships is a complex process, and the mistakes we make in conversation are often a reflection of our confusion about how to balance asking and telling (along with our bias toward telling) and how to ask in effective ways.

The missing ingredient in many conversations is curiosity, and we can overlook how important curiosity in another person can be in developing a good relationship (Guzman, 2022). We demonstrate curiosity by asking questions that we do not already know the answer to. The act of asking temporarily empowers the other person in a conversation and temporarily makes the asker vulnerable. This is because we have implied that the other person knows something that we do not and puts the other person into a position of agency in a situation. A conversation that leads to a relationship has to be balanced and equitable, and so we need to invest something into forming that relationship. That investment is usually made in terms of attention, and by asking a good question a citizen shows that they are prepared to listen (and is thus invested). We build trust when one person makes themselves vulnerable/humble, and the other person sees themselves as having something of value to contribute. Radical civility rests on practices of humble inquiry by building relationships based on curiosity and interest in the other person, and by empowering the other to build trust.

Much of what comes next in this book is designed to help facilitate connection-building, not instrumental persuasion. Radical civility asks us to try to connect before we try to convince, to improve the relationship at stake in the interaction. Even in circumstances where you despise a person's beliefs or attitudes, seeking to connect with that person might just unlock a new path forward for both of you. This means sharing your story and hearing theirs, and it also means asking questions that will draw them into conversation by giving them agency. If we always seek to connect before we convince, then we'll have better relationships and be in a better position to make change in the world. A focus on instrumental forms of persuasion simply doesn't afford us the same opportunities.

Principle # 2 – Treat Other People as Multi-dimensional and Capable of Change

We've all heard, since childhood, that stereotypes are bad and that we shouldn't stereotype others. But stereotyping is something that human brains do automatically – they jump from visible or known qualities of people and things to assumptions about them (Oakes and Haslam, 1994). In everyday interactions with the world, this is very helpful. With doors, you probably have a useful stereotype that you turn the handle left (or push the lever down) to open the door. Ninety-nine percent of the time you'll be right. But then there is the moment in a public building where you're faced with a glass door and you have to decide whether it's a pull or push. You have some ideas ("push when you are leaving the building") but that isn't always right, depending on the setting. You look to see what others are doing, and look to see if the doors are marked, and so on.

The same thing happens when you engage other people; your mind may instantly jump to assumptions about them, but you have to slow down and ask yourself if those assumptions match reality. You know – because you've been told since childhood – that they almost certainly don't. Our questions are these:

> Why *are* stereotypes wrong?
> What do you have to *do* to resist them effectively?

First, the reason stereotypes are wrong is that people are complex; they can't be reduced to a type or a one-dimensional description ("He is just a ...."). Each person is a specific individual, with a personal history, experiences, thoughts, education, feelings, and so on. This has to be a stance that you take with people in order to practice radical civility. It's not based on prior knowledge about the person or deciding which people are complex and which are not (that's a stereotype itself!). It's also not based on reciprocity, where you treat people as complex only if they are treating you that way; if you always take this stance, your communication may start out being asymmetrical.

To be honest, this commitment requires work and effort. It is easier, in the moment, to just reach into your automatic responses for "this kind of person" and never find out who they actually are. Sometimes that might be ok, but it doesn't work in general. You can't build an authentic relationship with a stereotype. And if you think about a time that you were stereotyped, you probably didn't like it: it's insulting and probably makes you actively dislike the person who does it to you. The Golden Rule applies here. What does it mean to take the stance that people are multi-dimensional? Do a little experiment in your head.

> "Picture a _____."
> (Fill in with republican/democrat/farmer/coder/man/woman/construction worker/LGBT/mom/teen, etc.)

Really fast – what do you see? Probably you think of this particular label as a fixed identity, not as that person sees it and not as one of many ways that person could see themselves. We might imagine they have a limited set of values and weak skills of reasoning (we often see others as more gullible and easily taken in than ourselves). We may even think this person has a skewed view of reality, and the politics to go with it. If our interaction with the person is pretty ordinary, maybe this doesn't matter too much. But when we have to build a more substantive relationship, and especially work through differences or conflict, the results of stereotyping can be explosive. When we see people simplistically ("you're just a ____"), we are more likely to react with anger to what they say and less able to build trust with them. We may mishear or misunderstand things people say to us, because we hear them through the filter of a stereotype.

What's the opposite? How do we create, intentionally, a complex and authentic picture of a person? Let's look at some specific tactics we can use to remind ourselves how to engage someone authentically. The great American poet Walt Whitman once said, in *A Song of Myself*,

> Do I contradict myself?
> Very well then I contradict myself,
> (I am large, I contain multitudes.)

We can take two lessons from Whitman. First, we all have some contradictory beliefs, and we are going to be inconsistent sometimes. That's ok, since it just means that you are engaged enough to get into the complexity of experience. Second, no one is monolithic, even if they sometimes pretend that they are. We are all a jumble of complex thoughts, beliefs, values, hopes, and fears, many of which are in tension with each other. Proponents of motivational interviewing (Miller and Rollnick, 2012) (a longstanding, widely tested method of communication used for changing beliefs and behaviors) teach people to listen for ambiguity in others, expecting it to be there given how ordinary it is for people to hold competing or conflicting beliefs and opinions. We respond differently to different issues; we don't have to stick to a single story to explain our lives (like "it's all about money" or "people are just in it for themselves" or "people are mostly good"). How can we turn acknowledging complexity and inconsistency into techniques for interacting with others? We should always be suspicious of our tendency to see someone as simple, and equally suspicious of their self-presentation as one-dimensional. The remedy is asking questions, and really listening to the answers, not listening to refute but to understand. If we ask people to explain or justify their beliefs or actions, it can provoke defensiveness. If we make supportive inquiries ("Help me understand," "Tell me your story," "This seems important to you"), the ensuing conversation will start to reveal some complexity, and allow you to do so, in a non-threatening way. When we listen in those ways, we might hear a person express ambiguity or uncertainty, and that is an opening to a constructive conversation.

One of the things we find out if we actually embrace the complexity of another person is that they do or believe things we don't like and may even find abhorrent. What do we do with that? Do we hold the person to account for their worst beliefs and actions, and shun or condemn them? Or do we take into account the total person, the parts we find good as well as bad, and decide we can work with the good to understand and maybe change the bad? While there is a time and place for the former, it results in a broken relationship. The more accepting stance ("This person's glass is more than half full!") results in a relationship that might have some productive conflict, leading to a greater understanding of both differences and common concerns and allowing people to work together effectively.

A surprising fact is that, actually, we all share almost all of our values – we just prioritize them differently or understand them in different, complex ways. Really, everybody values

- Family
- Freedom
- Security
- Loyalty
- Intelligence
- Generosity
- Creativity
- Humanity
- Success
- Respect
- Health
- Cooperation
- Trust

And many more. Where we get into disagreements is when the values conflict; conflicts between values often lie at the heart of conflicts between people. Famously, Benjamin Franklin wrote: "Those who would give up essential Liberty, to purchase a little temporary Safety, deserve neither Liberty nor Safety." Here he makes a statement about how these values should be prioritized (but doesn't reject either value), but there are certainly situations where you could argue the opposite. Recognizing how many disagreements are about the (honestly complicated) problem of balancing different values should help us remember that other people aren't necessarily evil when we disagree. If someone, for example, values money more than health, it doesn't follow that they are a greedy, terrible person. We should be trying to find out what the real story is about this priority: Is it explicit and understood? Was there a process to get to it? Does this person see upsides to it that we don't?

The things we believe and do can have different levels of what you might call "commitment." Some things we say and do are mostly in the moment, responding to a particular person or choice; we aren't particularly committed to them. Some things we say and do are much more meaningful and durable for us, we have a serious commitment to them. Understanding the complexity of another person will require figuring out what beliefs are commitments and which ones aren't. Sometimes people will say things, especially in an online context, just to get a rise out of someone ("trolling"). On the one hand, they may have no particular commitment to the obnoxious or absurd post, and maybe it's best not to engage in it. But on the other hand, we need to really find out how committed they are to trolling, which is an inauthentic and aggressive way to engage others.

The linguist George Lakoff (2016) proposed that Americans generally view government and public life through one of two frames, which he calls "strict father" and "nurturant parent." By a *frame* he means a general metaphor or story for interpreting events. He's trying to explain why people can look at the same event – 9/11, any presidential election, the COVID-19 quarantine of 2020 – and have totally different reactions. Different facts? Maybe, but usually it's because they frame it differently. When we disagree with someone, how much is a frame disagreement, and how much is about the facts or issues? Lakoff thinks that we all buy into a metaphor of the nation as a family, but we frame the values and actions of "family" quite differently. Conservatives tend to favor the "strict father" frame, which positions people as independent agents who need strong values, self-reliance, and self-control, to keep them from laziness, cowardice, or behaviors of excess (like addictions); this frame sees people as born wanting to do what feels good, not what is right. What's required is an outside force to create boundaries and consequences, to discipline and maybe punish people to keep them on the straight and narrow. This frames most public issues as problems of personal responsibility and values liberty and choice over almost everything else. The opposing frame, the nurturant parent, sees people as in need of support for the overall goal of growth and fulfillment and begins from the assumption that people have a right to the things that will help them flourish (Recovery Village, 2022). Public issues get framed in terms of systemic, rather than personal, failures to support people. Consider addiction:

> Is it the result of the addict's series of bad choices and failure to be disciplined enough, which could only be encouraged by making drugs illegal and putting addicts in prison?

or

Is addiction the result of the inherent relationship of people and substances, and the lack of systems to help people in coming to terms with their addiction and support them in moving to a more productive life?

Civility requires everyone to be self-aware enough to see that problems can make sense within both frames, depending on the situation. We have to ask, in a heated disagreement, whether we can empathize with the other frame, without having to accept it. That empathy is a huge part of seeing the other person as complex and fully human. It's a little like the traditional Taoist image for yin-yang: a circle, with black and white halves that not only fit into each other at the tails, but also there's a white dot in the black side, and a black dot in the white side. If you can find yourself, even a bit, in the other side, it makes you see the other person differently, even if you think their frame is wrong.

Changing people's minds doesn't have to be your goal in engaging someone on public issues, but it might be an outcome of an ongoing conversation that doesn't have change as a goal. Sounds like a paradox, and in a way it is. What makes people open to change? First remember that no one should expect total conversion, a 180° about face. Instead, and quite reasonably, people change their minds by degrees. How? First, by establishing points of contact, things you agree about even if they have nothing to do with the issues at hand. Maybe you like the same kind of movies or art, have traveled to similar places, or share common frustrations about job/career. It doesn't really matter, because the more points of contact you have, the harder it is to see – and be seen! – as the evil "other." If you don't like people in a different party or religion, humanize them by talking about the easy parts before the hard parts. If they love knitting or stock car racing, and you don't, ask questions and find out how and why it's exciting or satisfying, and what role it plays in their life and family. This doesn't have to be, or seem, strategic. Just engage and see where it goes. You may spend a lot of time on this, but the investment pays off if for nothing else, you have a friend to disagree with – civilly.

You'll probably start to notice in exploring each other's lives and thinking, you'll hit on common experiences and values. Talking about shared values is important, because they can be hard to see in the heat of a moment. These points of leverage can change either or both of you. You might find yourself slowly in more sympathy with a policy you previously sneered at because you realize it is actually pretty consistent with one of your values, just not the one you thought. And your friend might have the same experience. The key thing is not to take a stance of manipulation, hoping for any specific outcome (including that *your* mind won't change). There is an old saying that the best persuasion is self-persuasion; we all, at some point, make a decision to change our minds, sometimes after a lengthy internal conversation. In the end, however, you have to count your relationship successful if you can just find the other person reasonable, even with your strong disagreement.

A member of Civility First, a non-profit organization in Washington State that aims to bridge political differences, told us a story about her experience running a dance collective during the COVID-19 pandemic. One of the dancers she worked with was anti-vaccine and anti-mask, and this was how she identified herself to the leader of the dance collective. The dance studio had a mask policy in place, and this particular person decided not to attend because she refused to wear a mask. But the leader of the collective missed the contributions this one person was able to make, so she decided to message her and this is what she said: "We really miss you and I wish you could dance with us. And I wish I could understand how you're thinking about this more." Without disclosing more information, the dancer returned to the studio wearing a mask a couple of weeks later. But that wasn't the end of the story. The dancer had applied for an exemption, which the studio denied. She then asked the group if they were okay with her being in the studio without a mask. The leader of the group said no and explained her reasons. In this case, the leader of the collective decided to lean into the complexity of the situation and the complexity of the person she was responding to. This meant navigating the conflicting desire to have this dancer be part of the group, the wish to respect the dancer's concerns and beliefs about mask-wearing, the safety of the group and the family members of the group practicing together, and the uncertainties of the situation itself.

What happened? They eventually reached a compromise whereby the dancer would wear a mask but would not practice "full-out" because she doesn't feel safe doing certain moves with a mask on. If we put aside our need to be right or wrong in this case and focus instead on the ways in which different, competing values are being weighed against one another and people are being asked to live within different degrees of complexity, then we get a sense of how to treat other people as multi-dimensional. The leader of the dance collective did not stereotype the dancer (although she easily could have). Instead, she tried to understand the complex reasons that may have brought her to those beliefs. This opened a space for the two of them to understand one another. This kind of example shows the promise of radical civility in action.

Acknowledging, respecting, and responding to another person's complexity can be one of the hardest communication challenges we face in day-to-day circumstances. We readily and easily reduce people to one or two beliefs and actions so that we can orient ourselves in any situation and make quick decisions about who's wrong and who's right and what the best course of action happens to be. But our tendency to do this reductive work in the interests of expediency almost always harms relationships. A willingness to see, and engage with, another person's complexity takes more time and discipline than we can feel that we have. But that time and discipline are essential for cooperative change to take place, the kind of change that can leave all parties involved feeling better (not one party feeling like a loser and the other a winner). That's what happened with this dance collective. Finding common ground took time, but everyone felt heard, understood, and comfortable with the outcome.

Principle #3 – Lean into Hard Conversations and Practice Self-discipline Even When It's Uncomfortable

The third principle of radical civility gets to the core of what's different between the three versions of civility we articulated in Chapter 1. This is not some kind of simple politeness or mechanism for avoiding the most important and divisive conversations in our lives. Radical civility asks that we lean into hard conversations, that we embrace the challenge of negotiating our deepest differences, and that we acknowledge that those difficult conversations are the sites of change. To do this kind of communicative labor, we need to be disciplined because difficult conversations can be emotional, can trigger people's reactivity, and can escalate quickly to conflicts. In the next two parts of this book, we'll lay out several specific communicative actions that can help people navigate the complexity of hard conversations. For now, we want to focus on what makes these conversations difficult, what some signs of breaking this principle look like, what some signs of a willingness to participate in difficult conversations look like, and an example of the benefits of abiding by this principle.

Daniel Kahneman (2013) makes a useful and important distinction between what he calls System 1 and System 2 thinking. System 1 thinking operates very quickly, with very little effort and very little sense of control. We learn how to make quick associations within System 1, and these associations can be helpful in guiding our decisions and judgments. But System 1 thinking can also lead us to jump to conclusions, oversimplify a complex situation, or activate our biases. System 2 thinking, meanwhile, is slower because it involves attention and effort. The operations of System 2 involve concentration, choice, and deliberation (as we'll see in the next section, deliberation is an achievement of radical civility). Kahneman's distinction can help us recognize the potential difficulty of some conversations. If we think about communication as a process of producing effects on others, one of the central axioms of communication is that one cannot *not* communicate because one is always producing effects on others. This means that there can be automatic, un-reflective, responses to what we say, how we hold our bodies, what we look like, etc. This is System 1 thinking at work, guiding a person's response to us without any deliberate thought. Here is the danger: engage someone on a controversial topic or an issue that they believe deeply about and you may risk activating the System 1 biases in their thinking. But this principle of radical civility asks that we lean into hard conversations, so we ought to recognize how those conversations lend themselves to automatic responses, physiological reactions, and biased thinking. Leaning into hard conversations requires that we make sure we are communicating with our interlocutor's System 2 and not their System 1; this will make for a more deliberate and slower conversation. That means we ought to be paying attention to whether our conversations are residing in a System 1 space of reactivity or a System 2 space of deliberate and careful thought. We want and need difficult conversations to be careful if we are going to practice radical civility.

Difficult conversations also come with strong emotions. Resentment, anger, fear, panic, frustration, we can see these emotions on people from all parts of the political spectrum when hot button topics come up. Usually, these emotions are strongest when the conversational stakes are highest. Not only, therefore, do we need to confront the problem of System 1 thinking, we also need to recognize how emotional people can be about difficult topics. These emotions inevitably bias our reasoning and make it harder for us to move into System 2 thinking. We don't want to court or engage with these intense, deeply held, negative emotions because we are worried that they will be painful or uncomfortable for us. Weak civility would lead us to avoid such emotions in the interests of superficial social harmony. Radical civility teaches us to look out for those emotions and lean into the conversations most likely to produce that kind of intensity. In communication studies, we call the desire to avoid conversation "flight behavior." Flight behavior is the intentional decision to avoid engaging with another person out of a fear that the topic might be dangerous or the conversation might pose a threat to us. If you see a group of people working collaboratively on a project and one person is sitting off to the side with their earbuds in, that person is engaged in flight behavior – they are intentionally ignoring the group and opting out of the interaction. The most extreme version of this is called "stonewalling," whereby one partner in an interpersonal interaction is intentionally unresponsive, tunes out, and turns away from a partner who is asking for engagement (Gottman, 1995). These kinds of communication practices cause resentment and hostility between people, but they can also feel like our best option if we know a conversation will be emotionally charged and difficult. Difficult conversations can too easily slide into contempt for the other person, which we want to avoid.

What do we do, then, to lean into hard conversations? Let's consider the important difference between responding to someone and reacting to them. This distinction will draw attention to one's own individual feelings and the feelings of others. If we are reacting, we are guided by our emotions and our System 1 thinking. If our ideas are challenged, let's say someone calls our interest in progressive taxation "socialism," we might react defensively by arguing that such a label is hyperbolic and inaccurate. To react defensively is common when we are being attacked, it is a natural reaction. But we are still operating in a System 1 space if we react defensively, and we initiate a cycle of communication whereby one side attacks and another defends and conflict grows. That's just what we want to avoid. Responding requires that we deliberately and carefully think about a person's claim *and* how we might engage with that claim in a way that doesn't trigger further emotions or that doesn't spiral into a back-and-forth of attack and defense. Responding means identi-fying the emotions behind our conversational partner's statement, the context within which it was made, and the intentions and hopes of what might happen with such a comment. So we may respond to the charge of "communism" by saying something like:

> That word seems to have some really negative connotations for you and you seem a little angry just saying it. I'm not sure it's a fair description of what I'm suggesting but I'm happy to hear more about why you chose that word.

Such a response holds the potential to pivot the conversation from a cycle of reactivity toward deliberative, careful talk. Of course, it might not work right away. You might get more vitriol and more snark back because the person you're talking to is still feeling reactive and is still operating in a System 1 way. But you've avoided the cycle of escalating emotions for the moment and you are leaning into a difficult conversation.

The best way to engage others in difficult conversations is to realize emo-tions are unavoidable and that we have a communicative responsibility to absorb, diffuse, or suspend intense emotions if we hope to engage in radical civility. Imagine being at a meeting whereby a topic on the agenda suddenly makes several people angry. Some heated conversation begins to unfold, you can see people's reactivity heighten and their System 1 thinking take over. What is your responsibility in such a meeting as a practitioner of radical civility? You could table the topic and suggest the group come back to it at some other point, but this is flight behavior. Instead, you need to find ways to absorb or diffuse the emotions in the room, perhaps by active listening (which we'll learn about in the next section), emotional labeling, asking open-ended questions, or acknowledging the feelings and thoughts of the people reacting strongly. These responses will help guide the conversation to a more careful and reflective space instead of a reactive and emotional space. Once people slow down, visibly begin to think and consider what's being said, then you know you've flipped the conversation to System 2 thinking. Too often we don't take the time to work past emotions, to let them be absorbed or dif-fused, so that we can reach a more productive space of engagement; radical civility asks that we don't run from those emotions but that we go through them, acknowledging them, allowing them to exist however they need to, and ultimately absorbing them in ways that can lead the conversation back to productive and constructive grounds and away from overly emotional and reactive grounds.

The president of Civility First told us she was at a city council meeting in Langley, Washington. Since the meeting involved a conversation about gun control laws, several people were there with firearms to (they said) advocate for their Second Amendment rights (and against some proposed legislation). The meeting itself was productive, but afterward, in the parking lot, a man with a firearm began yelling at an older woman who had testified in front of the city council. This woman was terrified, frozen in fear. The man was visibly angry, yelling and pointing his gun at her. This was a reactive situation where emotions were in control. The president of Civility First moved to stand between the man and the woman and said calmly: "You realize that she cannot hear you." That caused the man to stop for a second; it was as if something short-circuited in him for a moment. He stopped yelling, then asked: "So what's the issue then?" He seemed confused by why he himself was so upset. The president of Civility First had the courage to lean into a hard conversation but also had the self-awareness to know that emotions were making any form of engagement impossible. She did not react to the man with anger (or with any emotion really), and instead she calmly pointed out a fact (it's hard to be heard when you are yelling and threatening someone). This neutrality absorbed some of the man's emotions and pivoted the conversation to a different direction. Nothing particularly productive could be gained from that parking lot inter-action, and the man eventually stormed off (he was likely too emotionally charged to really deliberate in that space anyway), but the ways in which emotional regulation can influence difficult conversations were clearly on display.

If we're going to practice radical civility and lean into difficult conversations, we need to do it in just the manner that the president of Civility First did it, in as neutral and objective a manner as possible in an effort to absorb and diffuse as much of the emotion in a difficult situation as possible so that we can find a constructive space to engage people. We cannot hear people that are yelling at us because their yelling causes an emotional response in us that prevents us from being careful and deliberate. Too often difficult conversations start with, or move to, yelling really quickly. That doesn't mean we should avoid those conversations; it actually means those are the conversations we ought to be having. But it does mean that we need to practice self-control when engaging others around such issues and that self-control is both a matter of keeping oneself in a neutral, non-reactive space and absorbing or diffusing the emotions of others. It also means looking for signs of a move from System 1 to System 2 thinking and knowing that some of us have a responsibility, if we are to manage difference well, to do the hard communicative labor that comes with difficult conversations. We admire the president of Civility First and her willingness to do that communicative labor, even if it might not have resulted in a constructive outcome in that case. If we remain outcome indifferent and focus instead on leaning into hard conversations in ways that move us past the initial kinds of emotional reactivity, then we know we've done important relationship building work. If we can have these kinds of difficult conversations without them spiraling into attack–defense cycles, then we know we've managed to develop a bond with another person, whether or not we come to some kind of agreement at the end. That is the payoff of practicing this principle of radical civility.

Put these three principles together and you will be able to form durable, connected relationships with strangers. You'll also have opened up the possibility of change or transformation, either changes in beliefs or behaviors. These principles will help stitch together a social fabric in a democracy, and that social fabric will be strong enough to handle change and support good decisions. If the social fabric is built by emotional, System 1 thinking, instrumental approaches to persuasion and manipulation, and assumptions about others that reduce people to simple caricatures, then we cannot have a thriving, multi-cultural democracy. The key now is to turn these principles into a working process and an effective set of practices.

3 The Process

How do we go about living by the three principles of radical civility that we just described? These three dimensions are all necessary components for practicing radical civility; they make up the core features of a conversation that can be characterized as radically civil and that can embody the principles laid out in the last section. If you are a participant in a conversation where each of these dimensions is present, then you know you are on your way to building a durable and meaningful relationship and that you've done some work in weaving together the social fabric of democracy.

Dimension #1 – Active/Deep Listening

All of our interactions with others are a delicate dance, and they need to start off on the right foot in order to succeed. Starting right requires listening. Active listening is the necessary starting point for radical civility because it opens the possibility for connecting with others, for understanding others, and for leaning into constructive and difficult conversations. But it's not just a first dimension, it's always part of the process we lean on, and go back to, whenever the conversational going gets tough. We cannot treat others with civility if we are not curious about their views, ideas, feelings, or commitments. Curiosity can fuel and drive effective conversations much more powerfully than declarative statements or partisan attack-and-defense tactics.

Radical civility, as we've said already, is not a matter of etiquette or manners; we're not talking about the kind of listening where we nod our heads while we think of our next line of attack against our conversational opponent. We think of civility as what's necessary to stay in tough conversations and connect under conditions of difference. Not any form of listening will do for such a task. Active listening is not a matter of politely waiting for your turn to talk or listening to your neighbor drone on about their frustrations with your neighborhood rules or bylaws. Most of us are too eager to talk. We think of communication as the expression of our inner thoughts and beliefs and we miss the initial, and necessary, act of deeply listening to others. Of all the lessons in this book, this is perhaps the most important because if you never hear your conversational partner, it's unlikely that the communication habits

DOI: 10.4324/9781003442165-3

that follow will do all of the work that they can. The failure to listen has been exacerbated by the habits of interaction online and over social media. People want to destroy or cancel. The aim of argument on a Facebook thread is to end a disagreement with a winning, knock-out blow. Of course, this never happens. The aim of radical civility is first to connect before you try to convince, and that's why we must start with listening.

Active listening is more than just a polite social habit; it's a transformative communication practice. When we choose to listen deeply to someone else, we are choosing a way of responding that will improve mutual understanding. Too often we can be distracted, half-listening, or thinking intently on what we might say when it's our turn to talk. We might assume that we've heard what someone else is saying before and so our focus can meander elsewhere. These poor listening habits can make it harder to engage with, and understand, others. Active listening is a structured form of responding that heightens our attention to our conversational partner and allows us to enact the principles we've described above. When we practice listening in this way, we confirm that we have heard the person we are talking to. This does not mean that we agree with them; it simply means that we acknowledge their position, belief, or feeling. This has a powerful effect on others. It can help people move from a heightened state of tension or anxiety to a calmer state of comfort and security. It can transform hostility to mutual curiosity. And it can defuse the attack–defense cycle that many of our toxic conversations fall into.

The active listener takes care to attend fully to their partner's statements and repeats or mirrors the key elements of what's been said. We don't have to agree with our conversational partner, but we do have an obligation to rephrase what they've said so as to insure a shared understanding. The act of restating allows a speaker to find out whether the listener really understood what they had to say. If the listener did not, the speaker can explain some more. The active listener is not, however, just listening at the surface for the facts and reasons articulated by the speaker. The listener ought to interpret their conversational partner's words in terms of feelings. Thus, instead of just repeating what happened, the active listener might add context by identifying the feelings that the speaker is displaying. Then, the other partner can go beyond confirming that the listener understood what happened by indicating that the listener also understood the partner's psychological response to it. Here's an example: Let's say you have a stubborn teenager at home that doesn't like doing chores and is frustrated by remote, online learning. The teenager declares that she will not be doing the dishes tonight and is tired of living in a "dictatorship where parents get to decide everything." An active listener might say in response: "You clearly don't want to do the dishes tonight and you think this house is run like a dictatorship. Sounds like you are very frustrated and angry right now about the chores and how decisions are made here." Here the active listener has mirrored the teenager and added emotional context to check if they have understood. Laurence and Emily Alison argue that this kind of listening is the key to building rapport. They use it to train detectives how to interrogate suspected criminals. Anyone in a frantic, heightened state of emotion can be transformed by an effective act of mirroring or reflective listening.

Mirroring is one of the initial and most basic forms of active listening. Restating, summarizing, and reflecting another person's position are the heart of active listening. We can develop our commitment to active listening further though. As the previous example shows, we can engage in emotional labeling by putting feelings into words. To help begin with this task you can use soft and tentative openers. For example, you might say: "I'm sensing that you might be feeling worried (anxious, nervous, etc.)." A speaker might not be fully aware of the emotional content of what they are saying, and so emotional labeling shows that you are listening for that emotional content as well. We can also ask probing questions. These are questions designed to draw someone deeper and to explore more substantive and complex details, information, or concerns. For example, we might ask hypothetical questions: "What do you think might happen if you did X?" We could also validate a speaker by responding in an authentically interested way. You're trying to acknowledge the other person's thoughts, feelings, or experiences and empathically confirm the importance of a speaker's attempt to communicate those thoughts, feelings, or experiences. You might say: "I really appreciate your willingness to talk about this sensitive and difficult issue." We might also allow for comfortable silences that slow conversations down. Too often, especially in intense or heated moments of communication, we rush to say all that we wish to say. But an active listener is able to pause, handle silence well, and give their conversational partner time to think about what it is they are saying or what they want to say. Silence can also be very helpful in diffusing intense conversations that could potentially become overheated. Active listeners also use "I" statements and focus on the content of what a speaker says and not the character of the speaker. An "I-message" lets your conversational partner know how you feel and why and prevents the conversation from veering toward the "criticism-contempt-defensiveness" communicative cycle. In addition, you should avoid why questions (which tend to make people defensive), advising (offering your recommendations about what ought to happen), patronizing (looking down on a speaker), preaching (constantly using the word "should" to tell your conversational partner how they ought to act), and interrupting (this shows disinterest in another person's views).

The ability to engage in reflection, while maintaining a kind of neutral tone, is at the core of active listening. This means that reflection is both an attitude and a set of communication skills that we can use as a listener to help us understand and explore other people's thoughts or feelings. Reflection, and active listening more generally, allows us to see what lies beneath or beyond someone's initial statement. In communication, meaning is not just a matter of the literal words one person utters to another. Context, tone, figurative associations, all of these things matter in the process of making meaning and reflection can allow us to attune ourselves to what's beyond the literal, semantic content of a sentence. We don't think of this as the caricature of a therapist simply parroting back what their patient has said (answering, for example, a question like "What do you think?" with the question, "Well, what do *you* think?"). Reflection, and active listening, is a way of resisting the temptation to correct other people's thoughts, ideas, or feelings. We *can* use simple reflections by restating what someone has just said. The important thing when we listen in that kind of way is to select the correct word or phrase to reflect and emphasize. We can also use "on the one hand" reflections. This involves summarizing back to a person two conflicting views or conflicting emotions that they seem to be communicating. In doing that, however, we do not argue back. We can use reflection to ask for more evidence by reflecting part of what's been said and asking: "Can you tell me more about that?" We can also choose to pick out the positive in what's been said and reflect that positive back to our conversation partner. This is part of reflection as re-framing or paraphrasing what's been said in order to move conversations along to the next topic.

Active listening has several major benefits. First, it forces us all to listen attentively to others. Second, it avoids misunderstandings, as people have to confirm that they do really understand what the other person has said. Third, it tends to open people up, to get them to say more, and it leads to further disclosure. When people are in conflict, they often contradict each other, denying the opponent's description of a situation. This tends to make people defensive, and they will either lash out or withdraw and say nothing more. However, if they feel that their opponent is genuinely attuned to their concerns and wants to listen, they are likely to explain in detail what they feel and why. If both parties to a conflict do this, the chances of being able to develop a solution to their mutual problem become much greater. Fourth, active listening shows great respect to the speaker. It demonstrates an authentic interest in understanding your conversational partner's point of view, which greatly facilitates the development of a trusting relationship. Fifth, active listening allows us to spot flaws in a speaker's reasoning, it makes it easier for either conversational partner to consider alternatives to one's own narcissistic views, and it allows us to identify points of agreement within a conflict. All of these are ways of gaining a more substantive understanding of another person. In any case, active listening is a conscious skill that requires considerable practice to master. We can simply use a speaker's words, along with silence, concentration, patience, attentiveness, and some brief questions or restatements in order to draw someone closer.

The technique that we might call "image-response" is a more advanced form of active listening and requires careful phrasing on the part of the listening partner. When engaged in conversation with someone, inevitably whatever that other person says will produce an effect on the listener. One way to understand this effect is to pay attention to the image being created in the mind of the listener. For example, if my partner tells me a story about something that happened at work that day the story will likely have at least one signature image that affects me, as the listener, and draws my attention. An active listener reflects this image back to their conversation partner. It's important to note that this image may not be the same image that the speaker had intended from the story. In other words, this is not just a matter of mirroring words but actively reporting on the main effect of the speaker on a listener. I might say to my partner, "wow I can just see your boss's red face and how angry he must have been." This would be an authentic response by virtue of how I have reported on the main image (and hence effect) that I've taken from my partner's story or words. My partner might be surprised by my response, but something in her story or her multi-modal way of expressing that story made a particular impression. A good listener brings this to the attention of their conversational partner so that their partner is aware of the effect that they are having. An even more advanced form of this kind of listening requires that the listener articulate the deeper meaning or emotional value behind their partner's words in such a way that their partner wishes they could have articulated themselves. In other words, the "image-response" technique can quickly turn into the "deep-listener" technique whereby one partner seems to intuitively know and explain exactly what the other partner is trying to say with his or her story or anecdote. When the speaker or storyteller hears the deeper meaning of their words or story reflected back to themselves, then that speaker or storyteller will be drawn closer to the listener and feel a deeper intimacy, as if the listener "just gets" him or her. These forms of active listening go far beyond mirroring and require one partner to actively construct either the image or deeper meaning of another partner's words.

Taken together, all of these listening techniques are the best means we have for connecting with others, understanding others as complex people, and leaning into difficult conversations. This is probably the fundamental dimension in practicing radical civility and opens up the possibilities for what we describe in the other two dimensions. Without active listening, we descend into the cycles of violent attack and defense that we see play out on social media and all areas of our culture right now. These are not meant to be advanced or complicated communication practices. They can be mastered with a little practice and attention. They're also backed by decades of research. In other words, we know they work. Good hostage negotiators, good detectives, good doctors all use them to succeed in their professions. It's time that good citizens started using them as well to repair our broken public discourse, regardless of your political affiliation.

Saul Alinsky, the famous community organizer, trained many people in the practices of social movement building during the middle of the twentieth century. A core feature of all organizing aimed at building solidarity was the house meeting. These house meetings were an opportunity for professional social movement organizers to listen to members of a community as a necessary dimension in any form of political action. A house meeting is a small gathering of around 10–15 people who are invited to the home of someone they know and trust to discuss the issues that they face in their daily lives. The role of the organizer is not to advocate for policy positions or the goals of an organization; it is to solicit people's stories, to get to know people, and to listen deeply to people in a community. These meetings are necessary for trust-building if any movement is to be successful and they succeed or fail based on the listening skills of the organizer. An organizer able to actively listen as we've described above is always better able to build relationships and trust within the community. This means that community organizers, trained by Alinsky and others, would practice active listening as a necessary component of their political work. This is quite different from door knockers who come to our front doors soliciting support for a political candidate or cause by reciting what positions or policies they are advocating for. These house meetings are an excellent example of the work that active listening can do.

Dimension #2 – Managing Conversations

We've said a lot about why conversations are important, and now we turn to the mechanics of how you do them. Fair warning: A lot of what follows are things you know implicitly. Everybody is capable of carrying on a conversation in a range of situations, personal, professional, and so on. But this can get tricky when a conversation includes a huge disagreement or an "elephant" in the room, an issue that you don't quite know how to deal with because you're used to friendly conversations where you are both on the same page, and not that much is at stake. We can think of the skills of conversation as dividing into conversations drivers (opening things up), conversation maintenance (keeping things going), and conversation blockers (moves that shutdown conversation prematurely).

Conversation Drivers

Getting a conversation started is both simple and difficult: Ask a question, and then listen, really listen, to the answer. We covered listening in a previous section, so let's look at how to ask a good question. Good questions are ones that will open up dialogue without being threatening. If you ask a yes/no question, or one that has a correct answer, it can feel like being tested, and doesn't open a space for multiple opinions. Some questions that wouldn't (at least without a follow-up) might be:

> *Did you support the war in Afghanistan or not?*
> *Can you name the best movie of the last 10 years?*
> *Was the 2018 tax cut a bad idea?*

Of course, if the person hears the question as asking "and *why* did you think that?" then it's more like a dialogic question, but we can't assume that. Conversely, if you ask "Why did you support the war in Afghanistan?" it sounds not just like a test, but a little accusatory -- the question seems to presuppose that support requires some reasons.

Good questions, in this context, are *invitational* questions. Invitational questions do just that, they invite someone into a conversation, without presupposing how it will go. When you invite someone to a party, it's because you want to give them the opportunity to have a good time with others, not because there's just one thing you want them to do. Invitational questions can be reflective:

> *What did you think about the war in Afghanistan, or the US military abroad in general?*

You can replace "think" with "feel," and it's still an invitational question. Another strategy for being invitational could be pointing to a place and/or time:

> *Where were you when 9/11 happened?*

What's great about this question is that there are so many possible responses, from where in my life ("I was in college and …") to physically where ("I was in the car on the way to work when I heard…") to where in a political stance ("I was an isolationist coming into that day..."). Based on things the person has told you, you can frame questions in terms of narratives:

> *So, I guess you sing in a barbershop choir, that's fascinating, how did you get into that?*
> *Being a pediatric nurse seems like a real challenge -- what are things that most people don't understand about it?*

Almost any question that's a version of "Please tell me your story" is a great invitation, as long as it doesn't come from a place of negative judgement. (It's surprising how many questions, in a highly polarized context, can come off as some version of "What's the story about how you could be so dumb as to vote for our current legislator?", which obviously does not invite someone into a dialogue.)

Another kind of invitation to dialog isn't exactly a question but is similar. Sometimes you feel flummoxed by another person's point of view, and either you just don't get it or they seem to be repeating the words without explaining. Then you can try a formula like "Help me understand _____." This phrasing does triple duty. First, it indicates your interest and motivation to understand the other person. Second, it shows a vulnerability ("I'm having trouble understanding…") that can reduce defensiveness on the other person's part. Finally, it can give you something to really listen to and open a space for new questions and exchanges. Our point here is that even if you're not forming a relationship that's completely new to both of you, it may still take some work to both understand each other's life experience and values, as well as get in the habit of asking and answering "deep" questions.

Conversation Maintenance

Once we've got the dialog going, how do we keep it going? We've all had the experience of a conversation going off the rails, and we don't mean so much misunderstanding each other (that's the work of the conversation and can be productive), but more getting angry and frustrated with each other, and damaging the trust that is necessary to talk about difficult things. Let's talk about some of the things you can do to keep the conversation going, and enjoyable, right through the rough spots.

The number one thing is probably expressions of gratitude and praise, thanking the person for whatever they offer to you -- information, insight, self-disclosure, a challenge to your beliefs – everything is grist for the conversation and worthy of appreciation. It's so easy for a disagreement about ideas to turn into conflict between people, and the quickest way to make it clear that you value the conversation is to thank and praise the person. When you respond by saying "thanks, that's wonderful," it should be clear in the moment that you are trying to value the person, even if you are about to disagree with what they said. Of course, you have to mean it, or it can sound sarcastic, which doesn't work (see Conversation Blockers, below). Even if what you've been offered is *really* challenging ("You're completely wrong about that!"), you can respond by saying "I appreciate you being candid with me, and I'm trying to understand what you are getting at."

You can practice this from the other direction as well, when you would like to say something challenging, framing it as a friendly challenge.

> *So I want to challenge you a bit here because I think you've just made an important point*
> *I'm going to be a little hard on you about that topic, ok?*
> *I'd like to push you a bit on what you just said because I think I'm not following you, all right?*

The "tag questions" at the end ("ok?") are important, because if you actually pause, the person might object, which suggests you should change tactics. This approach goes hand-in-hand with "I-language." "I-language" can be used in place of "you-language." If you want to say something that could be perceived as negative, insulting, or accusatory, talk about yourself, not the other person. Instead of "You don't have any evidence for that claim" say

"I'm struggling to see where the evidence for that claim is." Phrasing it about yourself gives the other person a chance to save face, or even say "OK, I don't have much evidence" without it seeming like you put them down.

Perception checking, which is so important to active listening, also helps keep the conversation going when things get sticky. "So I hear you saying that..." is really useful when you feel you are not in sync with the conversation but can't quite put your finger on what you are missing. You can also accomplish the same thing by framing a comment as a perception: "It's my perception that you've talked about the danger from vaccines, but not the benefits." The person has a chance to agree or say "No, I did talk about the benefits, and they are..." Another way to talk about perception is something like "Well, in my experience..." which is ok, since you are limiting what you say to your experience, but it can be really helpful to back that up by telling a story that illustrates your experience. You can even just tell the story. Stories can be fun, funny, and colorful and allow you to fill out the point you are trying to make.

Another useful technique that communication scholars use to track conversational development is self-disclosure. We can share with people our own perspective in an attempt to move the conversation along, but we need to do so by paying attention to some signposts. Self-disclosure needs to escalate in a reciprocal fashion in order to be certain that trust is growing between two people. Communication research suggests that there are four levels of self-disclosure: facts, thoughts, feelings, and needs. We cannot just express our needs or feelings to someone unless we've shared some facts and thoughts and they've shared facts and thoughts with us. This means a conversation might look something like this: "I grew up in New York, not far from the Great South Bay" – here, I've shared some facts about myself. I need to wait to see if my interlocutor then shares some facts about herself. If she does, then I can escalate to thoughts: "I didn't really like growing up in the suburbs, everything looked the same and it seemed so boring." Now I wait to hear if my partner will share their thoughts, and if they do I can share feelings: "I felt lonely and bored most of the time." Again, I wait to hear feelings from my conversational partner before I escalate: "I really needed more excitement and more of a challenge in my life, and that's why I moved to the city." If our conversational partner does not reciprocate at one level, then I know I cannot proceed and I need to share more facts or more thoughts or more feelings first. This can work for political conversations too: "This new vaccine uses messenger RNA." If I'm talking to someone opposed to the vaccine, I can just listen for some bit of information and if they share that information then I know it's safe to go to thoughts: "I generally trust science because we've had a lot of really impressive medical breakthroughs in the past few years." This might elicit some challenging thoughts from my interlocutor, but I can respond by escalating to feelings instead of arguing with her thoughts: "I worry a lot about my loved ones and would feel safer if they got vaccinated." Again, listen for feelings back and if you hear them try escalating to needs, but if not disclose some more feelings to see if your conversational partner will come along. The important point is that we do not need to agree or disagree with every bit of information or every thought or feeling. Instead, we share with one another and develop the conversation through the reciprocal exchange of self-disclosure.

Conversation Blockers

Just as we can pay careful attention to how we might start a conversation or keep it going, we ought to avoid the kinds of communication practices that can stop conversations in their tracks, erode trust, and strain relationships. These are conversational red flags that the practice of radical civility asks us to avoid. While we discussed the importance of open-ended questions as conversation drivers, hostile questions operate at the other end of the spectrum. We can cite lots of examples of hostile questions, but here are a few that are especially troubling: First, there are questions that ask you to agree with a negative statement. For example, someone might ask us: "Don't you think taxes are just burdensome and unfair?" This is a hostile question because it immediately implicates us in a controversial topic but in such a way that attack and defense are our only options. Second, questions that involve trigger words are usually hostile. A "trigger word" causes a strong reaction, a person uses one to stoke emotions. We might be asked: "Don't you think Biden is sabotaging U.S. interests by releasing that Russian prisoner?" Again, there's very little conversational room to maneuver, but the word "sabotage" is especially troubling because of the inflammatory work it is designed to do. Third, questions that seek additional information in a hostile tone. We might be asked something like: "How much more money would we need to spend in tax payer dollars in order to keep welfare afloat?" The hostile tone is important to the question because the information being requested is not designed to extend the conversation, and it's designed to press a particular point. Fourth, questions that test your knowledge by asking you to fill in some deficiency in what you've said. We might be asked: "Haven't you even considered the importance of personal freedom in making choices about healthcare?" These questions are designed to put us on the defensive and heighten the argumentative distance between us and our conversational partner. Any hostile question helps to manufacture tension and highlight differences, and thus they turn conversation into hostile argument or divisive attack-and-defense patterns.

Ad hominem attacks are also conversation blockers. These are simple to detect and widely prevalent in political and personal discourse. When we are attacked personally, we automatically get defensive. These can amount to simple insults like calling someone a fascist or more complex attacks on someone's credentials, intentions, or motives. When we attack a person we treat them with contempt, and often times we reduce that person to a stereotype or a caricature of who they really are. We discussed these kinds of reductive moves and how they violate the basic principles of radical civility, and when we use them in conversation, they tend to make any constructive dialogue impossible. Expressions of contempt for a person are especially corrosive to interpersonal relationships, and character attacks are the easiest way to demonstrate contempt for our interlocutor. Ad hominem attacks tend to initiate toxic communication cycles whereby we either defend ourselves from the attack which prompts further ad hominem attacks or we attack the character of the person making the attack (sometimes on the grounds that the ad hominem attack is, in itself, a sign that the person we are talking with is untrustworthy). This may be the simplest red flag in this book, and it may seem like something we've known since we were very young. But communication scholars have shown that despite the general knowledge that this is bad communication, we still use ad hominem attacks, especially when it comes to political conversation, all the time.

The next set of conversation blockers that we need to look out for are overgeneralizations, extreme comparisons, and hyperbole. Godwin's law is an internet adage that asserts that as an online discussion grows longer the likelihood that someone introduces a comparison to Nazis or Adolf Hitler approaches 1, or, in other words, the longer an online discussion goes the more certain we can be that an extreme comparison is inevitable. These kinds of exaggerations are intentional attempts to end conversation and opt out of meaningful, collaborative dialogue. They are used to heighten emotions, distract from more careful points, widen the gaps between points of view, and introduce extreme moral language into any topic. Anyone that has a Facebook account has surely seen these extreme comparisons used in the course of a series of comments to some original post. Hyperbole comes from the ancient Greek and meant to over-throw. It suggests that you've intentionally gone above and beyond what might be considered acceptable or reasonable in any given conversation. Someone that uses overgeneralizations does the same thing, a wanton attempt to exaggerate to such an extreme that no meaningful response is possible. Imagine someone tell you that *all* women are irrational or that *all* men are physically stronger than women. These kinds of overgeneralization are obviously and easily refuted, but their real damage comes from the ways in which they introduce a divisive and acrimonious tone to a conversation, pitting two people against one another and placing distance between conversational partners that cannot be traversed easily. We know when someone uses these conversation blockers that they don't really want to talk in any robust way; they are telling us that they want the conversation to stop because it is too difficult for them to carefully engage with a topic. We have a responsibility to avoid this conversation blockers if we want to create a meaningful connection with someone different from us.

People that react with anger or with moral absolutes and also intent on stopping conversation. A moral absolute is something like the suggestion that all forms of taxation are evil. When we add this extreme language to a conversation, we intend to signal our unwillingness to discuss something any further. If we really think that any form of taxation is evil, then we are saying that any conversation around taxation is off limits and that we will not engage with that kind of talk. When we get indignant or angry at a suggestion, we also mean to take that suggestion off the table for conversation. If my colleague says to me in a very angry tone that our campus's policies around mask wearing during the pandemic are morally wrong and endanger parts of the university community, then I know that colleague is not ready to talk about that issue in a careful and considered manner. The anger suggests that emotional reactivity will govern any conversation and get in the way of genuine dialogue. We should be wary of any claim that suggests something is "morally wrong," "absolutely wrong," "absolutely right," "unequivocally good," "perfectly true," "undisputable," "obviously right/wrong," just as we should be wary of people communicating with anger, or in an irritated or aggrieved manner. These are all signals that a person does not want a conversation but instead prefers a fight. That also means we have a responsibility as citizens that practice radical civility to avoid these kinds of conversational practices.

Dimension #3 – Be Deliberative

When we are engaged in conversations that include active listening and that are opened up and flowing in important ways (and we've avoided the kinds of conversation blockers that we've identified), then those conversations can become deliberative. Deliberation is a goal which can shape conversation; it includes learning about an issue, considering diverse points of view, talking with others, problem solving, making decisions, and reasoning carefully and collaboratively. We can engage in deliberation on public policies and issues, but we can also deliberate on our own about what car to buy, what class to take, or what movie to see. In any of these contexts, deliberation slows the pace of conversation and thought, so that we can reflect, think through things with consideration, and explore different options. Deliberative decisions are usually better decisions; deliberation is an important way we engage our thinking System 2, discussed in Chapter 2.

Radical civility is also a deliberative project because it provides the glue by which different people might engage in careful reasoning together. In some sense, if we see deliberation at work we can assume that radical civility is also at work to keep that conversation in the sweet spot of cooperation and collaboration. Think of deliberation as when we engage others in argumentation aimed at making a decision or a choice. Argumentation requires creating and maintaining a relationship in which offering and accepting and critiquing reasons, and evidence for a particular claim, is possible. Civility is what helps us create and maintain these relationships. While deliberation aims at choice, these choices can be for just one person ("Help me think about whether I should buy this house or not") or "us" choices ("Should our town really give such big tax breaks to businesses?"). Both kinds require civility, because deliberation works best when there is disagreement. In fact, the root of the word *discussion* means "to knock ideas/argument together" (it's related to the word *concussion*). Thus, we are defining argumentation in terms of relationships, ones in which there is enough trust and common reference points that participants can be moved by reason to offer arguments, contest them, and sometimes change their minds. Sometimes people assume this is a natural stance toward others ("We're all reasonable, right?") and sometimes it is, especially people of similar education and social background. But in fact in most cases, this kind of relationship, on any difficult topic, needs to be earned in just the ways we've discussed so far.

Let's think for a minute about the contexts of argumentation. Argument can't be reduced to one thing ("making a logical argument"); it happens in different contexts and relationships for different purposes. Even if we restrict our attention to argument that overall has a deliberative purpose, there are variations. First, we can distinguish between terminal and ongoing deliberations; terminal means "end," as in a decision has to be made at the end of the conversation. Ongoing means that even when a policy is settled by a government or organization, argument can continue; witness the ongoing arguments over abortion rights, which will continue regardless of laws or court rulings. Argumentation can be institutional; in your role as a worker or volunteer you may be engaging someone (as in the case above the dance group during the quarantine). Sometimes in organizations or government institutions, argument precedes voting, and the purpose of argument or debate is to help people make up their minds. That kind of debate may call upon an adversarial relationship, rather than a collaborative one, and parliamentary procedure is meant to define the responsibilities and limits of those relationships by defining how to do argument when two sides are presumed to agree about very little. If you are used to discussion and collaboration, parliamentary procedure can be very uncomfortable until you get used to it.

We've be leading up to the deliberative dimension of civil discussion because our focus is not on institutional or governmental settings (though of course those are important, especially if you're in them) but interpersonal conversations you have; sometimes these are with strangers (sitting on a bus, the person next to you strikes up of a conversation), with a social or work acquaintance (conversation in the break room), or with a friend or relative. No organization or institution sponsors these conversations, but they happen all the time. Why? Thanks to various kinds of media, we are all part of what you can call a *deliberative ecology* (Matthews, 2014). This ecology consists of people interconnected by media, who partially share information and arguments. It's as natural to most of us as breathing that we inhale the news, sometimes of the day, sometimes in a longer timeframe. We find out what happened and what people said about it, what others thought followed from it.

The media system is vast and deeply interconnected, but any given person is exposed to only a fraction of it. What kind of media?

Print (books, newspapers, magazines)
E-media (books, newspapers, magazines)
Online news and comment sites
Social media (Facebook, YouTube, TikTok, Instagram, etc.)

People produce, consume, and share all kinds of information, pictures, and video for all sorts of reasons. But a part of this system is used by people to advance thinking about public issues; they produce, consume, and share information in service of understanding what *we* should do. Consider gun ownership. You may think the laws are fine as they are or wish to make them stricter or looser. But maybe you're not sure. You can join "the discussion" just be doing some reading and watching some videos; based on these you start thinking about your place in the discussion and what you think – and how you'd defend what you think. That's the moment where argument enters, as you begin to construct arguments for yourself, observe how evidence is used, and what the implications of a position are.

Often, we go through this process without consciously thinking about it; the amount of information available and the number of issues mean that there are lots of things we ignore. When we engage someone about one of these public issues ("I think we should have restrictions on long rifles" "Well, I don't"), the conversation is deliberative because we are talking about a choice *we* (as an individual, a city, state, or country) should make. Even if we don't have the power to make this choice directly, eventually we'll vote for candidates, or on ballot measures, that will influence the outcome; we may also participate in civic life and politics in other ways that make a difference. So, the conversation of any two people doesn't change the country, millions of conversations do – and you are part of that. The better the conversations, the better the decisions and the richer our democracy.

A word of warning is in order here, however. While many parts of the deliberative ecology are reasonably civil, some parts are not. Of course, much of what's floating around isn't meant to be deliberative, even if it touches on public issues, politics, and politicians; it's just mocking and mean-spirited, or the work of committed fans. But there are other things that present themselves as part of the deliberative ecology which are uncivil. Obviously deciding what's uncivil is a judgment call on your part, but it's important that you continually question that. We all consume media that crosses lines sometimes; when incivility is closer to the core we should step away. For example, it's easy on YouTube to find videos of the genre "X crushes Y with one killer argument!". Maybe you can extract something from which you could put to use in a civil conversation. But probably it's not a great use of your time, since even if the argument is an actual one, it's meant for uncivil purposes (*crushing* and *killing*). Some very reputable news organizations regularly use headlines that aren't supported by the content of an article; some trade explicitly in fallacious arguments, rumors, and unfounded allegations. We commonly distinguish between news and opinion (though the lines have become blurred). You can learn interesting and important arguments from opinion pieces, but if they are encased in dripping contempt and mockery, you have to work to extract anything of value and even then it may be dubious.

Given how much arguments matter, what argument responsibilities do we have in conversation with others? First, remember that argument is often provisional and exploratory, and if your civil relationship is strong, you can try proposals and ideas out to explore the implications ("Suppose we banned automatic weapons for civilians? What's the downside?"). But even if you're exploring, you are responsible to come up with reasons that are relevant and plausible; that's not always easy, and it may be especially hard in the moment ("Let me do some research and get back to you"). While you are responsible for having reasons and evidence to back up your positions, that doesn't mean the other person "has" to back down if they falter or struggle to defend their side. Since the conversation, like the larger deliberation, is ongoing, you can leave things where they are and pick them up again. Civil conversations don't assume that anyone simply has to chair their mind at any time. While conversation as deliberative is a process, there do come moments (such right before you vote) where you have to weigh all the evidence and arguments you've heard and make up your mind as best you can, knowing that you may change it later as you learn new things.

4 The Practices

Now that we've been through the theory, how does it work in action? Each of the practices we'll discuss below is a concrete way of doing civility, not just having civil intentions or the "right" frame of mind. Civility is something we commit to doing, and we can get better at it with practice. We think this version of civility is a necessary part of living as a citizen in a large-scale multi-cultural democracy.

But we need to deal with one of the central paradoxes of civility first. While we want to cultivate a community with a functional level of civility, the most important person is the individual citizen. All of these practices are for you. You don't need to enforce civility with someone else, and you probably can't. You don't need to play "gotcha" with someone's uncivil behavior or attitudes – in fact, "gotcha" is uncivil by definition. The asymmetry between your behavior and others' behavior is a basic fact of human life, across contexts. Should you be honest if others aren't? Yes. Should you be ethical if others aren't? Yes. An important component of the 1960s civil rights movement, particularly in the wing led by Dr. Martin Luther King, was their commitment to non-violence, which is also a commitment to asymmetric behavior; they pledged to stand fast to non-violence even in the face of horrific violence (Chenoweth and Stephan, 2012). Dr. King was, in part, inspired by Mahatma Gandhi, who coined the phrase "An eye for an eye will leave the whole world blind" to express the futility of responding to anger with anger, to violence with violence. As you read through these practices, you may imagine situations and people you've encountered and think "Well, I'll be civil if they are." It's natural to feel this way, but if you're waiting for them and they are waiting for you, change never comes. Another quotation attributed to Gandhi illustrates the fundamental approach of civility: "Be the change you want to see in the world."

Practice 1: Start from a Position of Humble Inquiry, Seeking to Find Out What People Believe, Do, or Value

Principle – Connect before you try to convince or persuade
Dimension – Active/deep listening

We've all been there, in conversation, with the know-it-all, the person who is very sure of themselves, and asserts everything with an almost aggressive

DOI: 10.4324/9781003442165-4

certainty. This style of interaction can make you want to walk away. The strange thing is that this person may not realize they are doing it. To be honest, we all do it at times, especially when we are focused on ourselves, and our confidence in what we are saying. But why is this confidence (sometimes arrogance) so deadly to good dialog?

In 1961, the communication researcher Jack Gibb published an influential article on "defensive communication" (1961). His basic premise was that specific attitudes and behaviors create defensiveness in others. Everybody wants a chance to be right or to contribute and if others act as if there is nothing more to be said, any of us might react by feeling attacked, as if we were told our voice doesn't matter. We then become defensive and may in turn attack others. Gibb was researching best practices for getting groups to collaborate in problem-solving, and that's exactly the kind of deliberative cooperation that we associate with civility. Gibb summarized his findings in a table, which lists the attitudes and behaviors which foster either a defensive climate or a supportive one (See Table 4.1). We'll return to several of these, but for our purposes here the important contrast is between certainty and provisionalism. Why is this one important? Let's think about two pictures of what it means to know something. The first one is exclusive: If I have the right answer, you have the wrong one. When it comes to bus schedules or the numbers of pounds in a kilogram, that's a reasonable stance. But the really interesting problems of public and political life aren't like that. They call on multiple values and have numerous factual dimensions (i.e., we have to decide which facts are actually relevant to them). A second picture is where everyone only has partial knowledge. New knowledge or information would be additive rather than exclusive. Your opinion on a controversial issue may be well-thought out and deeply held – can you still acknowledge that your certainty about it should actually be provisional, that you should believe this until you find out more?

In the Buddhist scripture the *Tittha Sutta* (2012) (the "Bridging Verse"), the Buddha responded to his monks' concerns about the diversity of theologies and practices at that time with the parable of the Five Blind Men and

Table 4.1 Categories of Behavior Characteristic of Supportive and Defensive Climates in Small Groups

Defensive Climates	Supportive Climates
1. Evaluation	1. Description
2. Control	2. Problem orientation
3. Strategy	3. Spontaneity
4. Neutrality	4. Empathy
5. Superiority	5. Equality
6. Certainty	6. Provisionalism

the Elephant. Five blind men are led to an elephant and are asked to describe it. Each naturally grasps a different part of the elephant, and when asked to describe it reference what they have touched. The one touching the leg says an elephant is like a tree, the one touching the trunk says an elephant is like a giant snake, the one touching the end of the tail says an elephant is like a giant broom. Notice that they are all right, and yet they are all wrong too. An elephant is these things, but more than these things. In the parable, the men begin to fight, each thinking the others are lying. The Buddha comments,

> With regard to these things
> > they (the men) are attached —
> some contemplatives & brahmans.
> They quarrel & fight —
> > people seeing one side.

A provisional stance would prevent this problem. If you thought your ideas were right or true or justified *until* you found out more, you'd be open to seeking new information and perspectives. Just because you have strong commitments doesn't mean there are (important) things you don't know. We all have to cultivate this stance. Part of us reacts by thinking self-critically, "Oh no, what if I'm wrong? Am I stupid? Will others think I'm stupid?" The attitude of humble inquiry is always smart, even if people are surprised by it – they are also happy to be included in the conversation and have their contributions valued and not immediately rejected. You are talking to a person, and you have to acknowledge that, at minimum, you don't know this person's experience(s), what they mean, and how they connect to your experiences. You might be eager to find out how they see the world and why. That doesn't mean you'll immediately (or ever) agree with them, just that you'll take them seriously and try to see what can be added to your understanding.

We could also call humble inquiry *curiosity*. We can stay curious (and nonjudgmental) about others and allow ourselves into their lives and worlds. The Roman playwright Terence once said *Homo sum, humani nihil a me alienum puto* (I am human, nothing human is foreign to me), expressing a wish to understand that full tapestry of the human experience, which we all, as humans, could do. So how do you *do* curiosity and humble inquiry? Here are some suggestions.

1. Use open-ended questions. Open-ended questions aren't yes/no questions and don't limit what the person can say. "Should this be legal or not?" limits the answers to "legal" and "illegal," while an open-ended question opens possibilities and invites exploration, for example

   Tell me about...
   What's the story with...
   How have you dealt with...

Then actually wait for a rich response. These questions open up space for different views, and as you listen, try to listen for what resonates in their story rather than silently critiquing. You don't have to agree with everything, but you can choose to focus on agreement.

2. Avoid factive verbs. Linguists have identified a class of verbs as *factive*, which means they imply the existence of a fact. Factive verbs create a presupposition that there's something true and not debatable. Compare these two sentences:

   Chris believes skiing is dangerous.
   Chris realizes skiing is dangerous.

   In the case of *believes*, Chris might be wrong in his belief that skiing is dangerous, but in the case of *realizes* the sentence implies that there is a fact that skiing is dangerous and now Chris has "realized" that. The problem for dialogue arises when "facts" get inserted into the conversation through presupposition, and it's hard to challenge them. "Don't you realize that skiing is dangerous?" and "How can you ignore the dangers of skiing?" sound like real questions, but they are really just asserting that skiing is dangerous, and any attempt to answer it will get tangled – If you try to disagree by saying "I didn't realize that" you've just admitted that skiing is dangerous. Here's a brief list of factive verbs in English:

know	realize	be aware (of)
ignore	discover	be indifferent to
comprehend	regret	be glad that
learn	resent	
deplore		

   Non-factive verbs (*believe, think, seem, feel, appear*) make things you say relative to you, to your experience and perceptions. That allows room for multiple perceptions. If you are talking to someone asking these kinds of questions or making these kinds of statements, you can always (as a good listener) reflect them back in a more non-factive form, "So you feel skiing is dangerous," creating space for your perspective, "I don't find it that scary."

3. Don't worry about "weasel" words or hedges
   If you explore writing advice online, you can find many pages that advise you to stop using "weasel words." They will tell you that these are hedges that weaken the straightforward claims you are making and reduce your prose to mush. Maybe, but in a civil conversation, these turn out to be exactly what you need. You need to signal that you claims have limits and that you are open to hearing more. A brief list might include

A bit	Likely	Rather
Almost	Many	Relatively
As much as	May	Reasonably
Basically	Might	Seems
Can	Moderately	Some
Could	Most	Somehow
Fairly	Often	Somewhat
In a sense	Probably	Usually
Just	Quite	Virtually

These words express your humility. One might hesitate to use them, thinking "If I say probably, then they'll jump in and say 'Oh what about...'." If you are absolutely certain you are right, maybe that's threatening to you. But if you are having a conversation, it means you want to be open to adding to or modifying what you think, so probably *probably* is exactly right.

Practice 2: Seek to Understand Not to Defeat

Principle – Connect before you try to convince or persuade
Process – Active/deep listening

Most of us struggle not to see conversation and dialogue as a kind of game, and we end up trying to win. Many of us have a persistent worry, especially in difficult conversations, that we must not let them believe something or "get away with" something – or "win." Engaging in dialogue with another means surrendering control over the conversation, and over that person. When the stakes are low (talking about next year's prospects for your favorite sports team), this isn't scary. But when stakes are high, anxiety is real, especially given the increasing tendency toward seeing political and cultural events in an apocalyptic framework ("This is the end of democracy!" "They're taking our freedoms!" "The Constitution is at risk!") (Mixon and HopKins, 1989). Let's take a moment to think about what "winning" means.

Does winning mean coming out unchanged, without having reconsidered or maybe broadened your own views? That seems like it would be winning by not even playing the game, since even if you don't change your mind, authentic engagement requires at minimum using humble inquiry to explore other points of view. Does winning mean getting someone else to change their mind or admit doubt about their views or actions? That kind of winning is also not compatible with civil dialogue; part of our promise to each other as citizens is that we won't try to dominate or control others (Neufeld, 2022). People generally change their own minds, in their own way and own time – an old saying has it that "the best persuasion is self-persuasion" (Aronson, 1999). In general, the win/lose framework is toxic to relationships. Sure, we all have friends we like to have arguments, sometimes heated, over sports, media, and maybe politics, but they don't break the relationship because "friendly" arguments mean that no one has to walk away the humiliated loser. Even in those friendly arguments, we know that there are lines we cannot and should not cross. Competitive intercollegiate debate has winners and losers, but everybody understands the framework, judges decide who wins/loses, and there is always another round to rejoin the argument. But whether it's strangers or friends or relatives, the higher the stakes, the more likely that a win/lose orientation will sabotage the relationship and make continued talk difficult or impossible. As we mentioned in Part 2, the theologian James Carse developed the contrast between finite and infinite games. Finite games, he says, are those with rules, boundaries, judges/referees, and winners/losers. An infinite game is any mode of interaction that changes rules, plays with boundaries, and exists solely for the purpose of continuing the game; human life itself is the paradigmatic case of an infinite game (Carse, 3-10). Civil dialogue has much more in common with infinite games than finite games.

What is the purpose of civil engagement with someone on an important topic? Creating mutual understanding – of differences as well as commonalities. Physicist David Bohm has expanded philosopher Jürgen Habermas' idea that, paradoxically, the best strategy for a good conversation is to not have a strategy (Bohm, 2013). When nobody is attempting to control the dialogue, it will likely be most productive of understanding. These are not the easiest conversations (it's easier to have a familiar genre, like "Let's fight about the best baseball team right now"), but when the issue matters they will work best. Notice too, that if both people go into it saying "I just want to understand what you think and where you're coming from" they create the possibility of something new: "Where are *we* at with this issue?" Instead of back-and-forth jousting to establish who's the winner, they can create something new. A good image here is the potter's wheel, with a piece of clay spinning on it. What if two people have their hands on the clay, shaping it?

In that case, you really can't say which person created or caused the final shape of the pot; it was co-created by both people. A civil conversation, even a deep and serious one, is aimed at producing mutual understanding about an issue or topic. Will that change people? Very likely, since you will both enrich your understanding of another person as well as clear up misunderstandings about their ideas and the world they live in. The organization Braver Angels offers what they call "Depolarizing Within" workshops (https://braverangels.org/what-we-do/depolarizing-within) which aim to get participants in touch with assumptions and ways of talking that increase or perpetuate polarization. The outcome is often "Wow, we're more similar than I would have thought." That's a change that enhances continued dialogue.

How can you double-check yourself? You can take steps to make sure your conversations are more about understanding than winning:

1. Don't keep score

    We live in a world awash with attempts at persuasion and influence. Commercials and ads are everywhere, from movie theaters to social media to blogs and podcasts. It's easy to fall into thinking that's the point – you are giving away your attention or money or resisting giving away these things. We can all find it hard to relax into a relationship where the only demand on us is to be honestly and curiously engaged; not that this engagement is easy or effortless, just different. We have to be aware of when we fall into keeping score with another person. They might make a really good point, or tell you a story that really resonates, and you may think (without realizing it) "OK, one for them, now I need to do it too." You don't. You just need to be fully present in the conversation.

2. Stay aware of your feelings of shame and defensiveness

    We all have beliefs, values, and habits we are comfortable with. It's uncomfortable to talk to people whose beliefs, values, or habits are very different. Sometimes that's because they directly challenge us, and sometimes it's because we have legitimate mixed feelings about a topic ("I eat meat, but sometimes I'm uncomfortable with it, especially the factory farming of animals"). Most often because just being aware of the sincere difference makes us feel like we have to choose: "Who's right? Me or them?" As we've noted, the truth in complex issues isn't usually exclusive, so you don't have to choose. But in a more subtle way, this sets up a scorekeeping mentality. "Joan has made me uncomfortable, so I'll do the same to her." Before you go down this road, ask yourself whether it's a sincere and appropriate contribution, or if you are reacting to discomfort with how the conversation is making you feel.

3. Keep filters on

    If the conversation is truly working toward mutual understanding, much of our daily equipment for responding to people isn't helpful. Someone's experience is their experience, and in this case no good purpose is served by responding to someone with:

    You're wrong
    That's not true
    You don't know that
    Why would you say that?

    And similar things. If you're trying to insert yourself into someone's world, you might not like what you see. You may find things that you feel are wrong (morally), wrong (factually), or just weird and offensive to you. Civility requires you, in the moment, to just bracket that and listen. At some point when trust is established, you will be in a position to challenge some things, but that certainly can't be your first move. Beating up on what the person is sharing will never lead to them being in a position to change their mind, they will just become angry and resentful and maybe stop talking to you.

This is a really hard problem. Everyone knows where the slippery slopes are, and we want to slide down them: "Well if you believe that then you must approve of this other outrageous thing and it's unacceptable that anyone approve that." But until you know more, you don't actually know what the person thinks; not everyone will see the same chain of implications as you. Unquestionably, civility requires holding your responses in check, sometimes because it's not the time or the place, and sometimes you just need to know more. Even when you are very sure someone is wrong, they deserve an honest conversation. That's civility (Renkl, 2018).

4. Celebrate and praise moments of connection and understanding

A great way to develop a new habit is to reward yourself for it. In this case, you can do it in two ways. First is praising the other person for their contribution:

> *Thank you so much, that must have been hard to say...*
> *I really appreciate your support in talking this through...*
> *I never knew that, you've really opened my eyes...*

A second way is to celebrate the thing you are building together. This not only keeps you in the habit of focusing on it but helps you both review and shape it as you go on. For example:

> *I think it's great that we've whittled our real differences down to just these two things...*
> *I'm so happy we've agreed that each of our political parties is not evil, but just wrong part of the time...*

Difficult conversations are so much easier when people make their goodwill and learning explicit to each other.

Practice 3: Be a Relationship Crossing Guard

> *Principle – Connect before you try to convince or persuade*
> *Process – Keeping conversations going*

We can practice civility in relationships that are deep or shallow. Sometimes, we interact with people we barely know or only know in a limited way (from work or a hobby activity). Other times, it's medium close friends, very close friends, or family. We have different investments in these relationships, but to the extent we don't want to break them off, the practices of civility apply (and clearly they cross over quite a bit with politeness in many cases). The investment we have in the relationship may impact the kind and amount of work we're willing to put into civil dialogue with them. You can be civil with someone at work without it being appropriate (for reasons of time or context) to launch into a deeply authentic discussion, yet if you are (say) traveling together many hours in a car, your relationship may deepen quickly. Alternatively, many people find that deep discussions with relatives are difficult and have unexpected consequences, so they prefer to keep dinner-table talk of politics at a more superficially civil level. We want to consider briefly how you can make these decisions in an intentional and thoughtful way.

Relationships are created and maintained in two ways. First, by patterns of interaction: where, when, how often, what's normally said and done. Second, by sharing information about each other, and "getting to know" each other more and more. We'll focus for a moment on this second aspect of self-disclosure (Tardy and Smithson, 2018). You create different relationships, in different contexts and for different purposes, by sharing more or less about yourself, or maybe sharing different kinds of things. You can work with someone for years and never know if they have siblings but know all about the concerts they go to. If you have siblings, you're probably pretty aware of what they do for a living. If someone at work initiates a conversation about, for example, a political topic that you have strong feelings about. You can make different but perfectly civil choices at this point. You might not want to engage and react by saying "That's interesting" and repeat some version of that sentiment until they give up. If you have a friendly enough relationship, you might jokingly say "Thanks for sharing!" with a big smile, and the person will take the hint. If not, you can be more explicit, "I prefer to stick to best TikToks of the day, ok?" Or you may want to take up the discussion and say "Interesting, tell me why that's important to you." You signaled interest but framed it around that person's commitments and perceptions, not so much the truth of what they've said. If they take you up, great. See where it goes, given the time that you have to spend on it. You can use the same script for close friends or relatives; with them, you may have to think harder about how far things should go. Being civil means you should listen without expressing judgment, but it also includes saying when you're not comfortable going any further. "I think we've moved from policy to disagreeing about our religious traditions here, and I just don't think I'm comfortable with that conversation."

In those cases, you are pushing the relationship before the dialogue, choosing a level of engagement that allows you to preserve the relationship. In cases where do you do want to engage the person, you may end up in a difficult conversation. What are some things you can do that will allow you to preserve the relationship while getting to a deeper level of engagement? Here are three suggestions:

1. You can let the person know, explicitly and sometimes repeatedly, that criticizing their arguments or ideas is not an attack on them.
    I'm going to reserve the right to disagree here...
    I'm going to say something you'll probably find pretty challenging...
    I really want to engage what you just said, because I think it's our real point of disagreement.

Of course, people can tell that you are disagreeing or challenging them, but it's really easy for people to mistake that for attacking them as a person. By signaling that you are going to disagree or challenge, you are showing that you care for their feelings and that you intend your disagreement to be friendly and productive. These may seem like pat phrases, but they can work wonders.

2. You can also explicitly signal your own discomfort

> *Ok this is a hard one for me to hear*
> *Can you see why that provokes me a bit?*

This helps the other person see, at a confusing or intense point in a conversation, that you're struggling a bit. It may produce clarifications or reassurances that help your conversation keep moving forward.

3. As things get intense, you can defuse the tension without fully derailing the conversation

> *OK, so can we summarize what this was all about in the first place?*
> *Remind me, again, what the stakes are here? What is this really about?*

Conversations can and should wander a bit. Sometimes you've strayed down a side road and you find your way back. Sometimes things escalate to a point where you fear there is more heat than light in the conversation. For some people, it's easiest to break the tension and refocus with humor. Not hostile humor but fun verbal quips or pop culture references ("You are the Spock to my Kirk!"); the best choices are in-jokes specific to your relationship to that person; they cut the tension and reinforce the bond at the same time.

However, a deeper problem about civil communication lurks right here, and it's a really difficult one. This problem is about "the line": What is your line, and what do you do when someone crosses it? Everyone has one or more of them. Typically, the line is something said or believed that you regard as so offensive that you can't get past it. You have to think about what those things are and what your response will be. If someone uses language that seems sexist, racist, or ableist, you have to gauge both the intent and the severity, relative to your willingness to have no relationship with this person. It also depends on whether they say things that are objectionable to you in general ("I'm sympathetic to socialism") or say objectionable things about you ("You're just another lib"), which is not very civil, but you could have a good discussion by objecting to it. Some kinds of race-baiting and antisemitism may cross your line in a way that makes you give up on having a productive discussion (they can be productive, but you have to decide if that's right for you, Acho, 2020).

Everyone has a right to draw a line, when an intense conversation becomes triggering or threatening. If you are a minority/non-majority person/identity, even in the interests of civility it's not required that you engage others to educate them, at the cost of your time and energy. But if you do choose to sometimes – it *is* one of the adventures of a healthy, diverse society – you still have to be mindful of limits. In an increasingly polarized time, we all approach these limits more and more often, and it's wise to think explicitly about where your line is, and the trade-off in being very tough or very lax in what you'll tolerate.

What's the best way to handle line crossing? It's probably better to be more like a crossing guard than a police officer. Police officers are serious, threatening, and associated with enforcing norms and violence. Crossing guards are different. They rely on a common desire to keep pedestrians and cars safe, and they do it by gesturing to the safe zone (the crosswalk) and help coordinate who gets to go at a given time. What are the best practices for dialogic crossing guards?

- Act as if people had goodwill. Just as nobody wants an auto accident with a pedestrian, the people you talk to want to have a good conversation. When thing come up that make you prickly, try to make your default assumption that they mean well.
- Don't nitpick what people say or how they say it, unless it's extremely serious. Lots of things will come up that you won't agree with, but unless a real line is crossed, let it go in the interests of not eroding the relationship and the dialogue.
- Avoid shaming the other person, about their morals, intelligence, or anything else. When confronted with something you think is stupid, it can be hard not to say "Why don't I believe that? Because it's stupid." It's not only uncivil, in the moment this will inspire defensiveness, but in the long run will make it hard to have a trusting relationship.
- Set up agreements as you go along. When something comes up that bothers you, as a crossing guard you can say "Can we agree not to do that?" (it might be a certain word, quoting a particular source all the time, an argumentative move, or other things). Too many of these will just be cumbersome, but if you can clear a space for a conversation, do so. Remind the person of the agreements when necessary and revisit these agreements as needed.

Practice 4: Seek Pleasure in Connection, Not in Anger or Self-righteousness

Principle – Connect before you try to convince or persuade
Process – Keeping conversations going

People like playing games, especially games they can win. Our brains look for dopamine "hits" (chemical bursts of pleasure) and lots of things provide them, from a compliment from a friend to seeing you were included in a social media post. But winning is strong. From video games to card games, from one-armed bandits to board games, there seems to be a pleasure in play that could result in a win. In fact, video gambling seems to be addictive in the way that opiates are. When we go into civil conversations, it's natural that we want to "score points" on the other person or do other things that result in a feeling of self-congratulation, often at their expense. Obviously, trying to win and scoring points are not consistent with being civil to others. But how do we deal with this?

Let's first consider the biggest obstacle, derived from Daniel Kahneman's (2013) concept of "thinking fast and slow," referenced in Chapter 2. Kahneman, one of the most famous psychologists of the twentieth century, points out that our brains are set up to have a quick response mode and a slower response mode; he claims this makes sense from an evolutionary point of view but functional today as well. When you see a dog lunge at you, you have to decide *very* fast if it is friendly or hostile – that's thinking fast. But you will also have a chance to reflect on that experience and decide if there was anything you could have done differently to not be in that position. In our civil conversations, we can get triggered (as a kind of fast thinking reaction), feeling the anger rise almost instantly and provoking an uncivil response. Often that's not fair; we haven't heard the person out, and we haven't explored their version of events. The point here is there are a quick pleasure and a slow pleasure we can get from dialogue. The quick pleasure of the fast retort or put-down is real, but so is the slow pleasure of an authentic conversation and connection, even if it doesn't result in changing minds or changing the world at that point. Once you become aware of your tendency to snap back (whether at a tweet, a Facebook post, or a friend you're talking to), you can engage your slow mode and switch to a different kind of engagement. It takes a little discipline at first, because your brain may be saying "please, please please… stimulate me now!" but you are in charge, and you can make it wait. This slower pleasure is akin to Mihaly Csikszentmihalyi's (2008) concept of flow; if you can suppress your tendency to react, you position yourself to move into a state where the dialogue seems completely natural and flows effortlessly. We can all think of moments where we had conversations like that; they don't happen every time, but we can actively cultivate them so they happen more often.

So how do you actually manage taking more pleasure in the process than the outcome?

1. Often, we strike when we feel attacked, so monitor your feelings. Take a pause, a breath, and think about whether something you disagree with is really an attack or … just something you don't agree with. If you give up trying to persuade the person, or seeing yourself as the Defender of the Truth, it's easier to relax and engage in disagreement.
2. When you feel yourself struggling with wanting to be defensive, take a breath and try switching briefly to safe topics (weather, sports) and then go back. If you have been building your relationships, you should know what the safe topics are.
3. As you watch your reactions, you can (paradoxically) become more comfortable with being uncomfortable. Discomfort goes with authentic

dialogue, as it explores real and difficult differences. (Discomfort is, of course, different from being attacked or purposely insulted.)

4. When you notice your discomfort, try to find a way to use humor to defuse tension. It's ok to have fun.

5. A dialogue is a success even when – or especially when – you don't persuade the person or resolve the issue. You can reflect in satisfaction on what you're learning without having to change someone else.

6. Celebrate and praise the relationship and dialog frequently.
   - *Wow, we're really dealing with difficult stuff here*
   - *I'm so pleased you're willing to talk to me about contentious issues*
   - *I feel like we are both learning a lot here, which is progress*

Practice 5: Repair When you Need to, Focusing on Face Saving and De-escalation Rather than Provocations or Trolling

Principle – Connect before you try to convince or persuade
Process – Keeping conversations going

No matter how good your conversations are, if you are doing something authentic, there will be rough spots. We have been describing the ideal kind of civil dialogue (though we've acknowledged the challenges it faces) but that can make it sound like if you just take our ideas to heart things will always be smooth. They won't. (If it were easy, everyone would be doing it and we wouldn't need to write this book.) So, in addition to thinking about how to make civil dialogue work, we have to think about what to do when it doesn't. We've already talked about what to do when the other person is crossing a line, but we need to discuss what to do when you realize you have overstepped. The crucial thing to think for keeping relationships intact is face-saving. Face-saving (Metts and Cupach, 2008) means granting the other person a story in which they can have self-respect (i.e., the opposite of shaming) so you can keep talking, which gives you more chances to be heard. Table 4.2 identifies some common breakdowns and ways to repair them.

Practice 6: Return as Much as Possible to What's Local and Concrete; Avoid Generalities, Hyperbole, and Impossible, Abstract Cases

Principle – Treat other people as multi-dimensional and capable of change
Process – Engage in deliberation

Two temptations in civil conversation require us to be vigilant and disciplined, and they are related to each other. The first is the tendency to talk in

Table 4.2 Communication Breeches and Repairs

Breaches	Repairs
Insult	When it's clear you've offended someone, just apologize. Then, as appropriate, start a conversation about how it happened, what it tells you about the relationship, and how to avoid it in the future.
Talking at cross-purposes	When things escalate or get heated, take a moment – often – to step back and ask "Where are we? Are we even talking about that same thing?" Complex conversations are hard, and moving in two directions doesn't mean things have gone off the rails, just that you need a quick check to agree on what you *want* to be talking about.
Talking over someone	Apologize and refocus on listening. It's true, sometimes people take long turns and repeat themselves; we all do it when we feel strongly. Have patience.
Grandstanding	Grandstanding is a version of scoring, when someone announces a position or value to show moral superiority. You can usually tell you've done it by the reaction you get. You can then apologize and offer that it's something you feel deeply about.
Misunderstanding	Sometimes you just mishear someone or just assume they're talking about what's going on in your head and soon you're talking at cross-purposes. Stop, take a moment, and try to reconstruct what happened. It's always good to apologize and take responsibility by getting things on track again.
Didn't reach agreement	This was never likely or even the purpose of a conversation about a difficult topic. Yet many people can't let go of it, so it's good to bring things to a close by pointing out that disagreement is good, and you've made great progress toward understanding each other.

generalities, which makes complex issues obscure and hard to engage. The second is to go immediately to hard or impossible cases and then conclude the dialogue will inevitably fail.

We all tend to think in generalities; it's simpler and it's easier. What are generalities? They tend to start with *all, every, always, everybody, all the time,* etc.

All liberals are...
All conservatives are...
Every religion ...
People are always completely selfish...
Everybody hates weakness...

And this list doesn't even take into account that "liberal" and "conservative" are unhelpful generalizations (ask someone about their personal liberalism or conservatism to find out how complex these are). The problem with generalities is that they leave little space for another person's beliefs, values, and experiences. They are like stereotypes that prejudge a person's position and often result in attributing beliefs and values to them which they don't hold or want to defend. It's hard to have a conversation when you're stuck with a label. Two things will help you avoid this problem. First, *ask*. Assume, in your spirit of humble inquiry, that you don't really understand someone's politics or religious views or values until you ask some questions and listen to the answers. This includes asking people their understanding of your positions:

Help me understand what you think socialism is?
How would you explain libertarianism?
What makes your denomination different from other kinds of Christianity?
How do you understand the history of slavery in the US?

None of these should be "gotcha" questions ("ah HA – you are WRONG!") but genuine questions that allow you to explore that person's understanding. This means that quick and easy debates, where each side just attributes something to the other and then refutes, are off the table. Instead, you're going to do something that takes more time and hopefully happens over more than one conversation.

The second thing you can do is speak from your experience, while always acknowledging your experience is a very partial slice of reality. Seeing random things on TV or the internet doesn't really qualify as experience (though they can be part of something that "got me thinking" and contribute that way). As above, hedging and weasel-words are good

I think that...
It seems like...
I feel like it's...
From where I sit...

Remember that you might be wrong – and act like it, accepting gentle critique and pushback.

The other side of this practice is to stay grounded in the specifics of what you've decided to talk about. The temptation to catastrophize can be very strong. That's where you either pull up (unjustifiably) an implication from what someone said, or slide all the way down a slippery slope: *If you believe that, you're a* ____. Insert, *racist, Nazi, communist,* or any other derogatory term that's ready at hand. Maybe the person you're talking with does affiliate with fascism or white nationalism; don't assume that from a casual reference or a particular word choice. Ask questions and find out. Given your topic, start with easy cases, not the hardest ones. If you're talking about tradeoffs

between privacy and free speech, or general welfare versus individual liber-
ties, you can try to find some cases where you mostly agree on the tradeoffs ("Drivers should obey road signs and posted speeds most of the time")
before getting to cases that are really hard (vaccination). And if you never
get to the hardest cases, it's ok. Value the journey, not the destination. Most
importantly, just avoid beginning your sentences in some overly abstract and
general way, or just avoid words like: all, everyone, every, most, etc.

Practice 7: Focus on Conversation Drivers Not Conversation Blockers

Principle – Lean into hard conversations
Process – Keeping conversations going

As we discussed in Chapter 3, we can always find ways to open up and ener-
gize conversation and other habits that tend to shut it down. Let's explore
some of the *drivers* for good conversation and the things you do (intentionally
or not) that become *blockers of* good conversation.

Drivers

A driver is something that influences an outcome. In any situation, multiple
drivers will influence where things end up. To create an authentic and productive conversation, you can keep in mind these strategies:

Open-ended questions
    As you ask questions (and you *should* ask questions and listen to the
answers), keep in mind that you want to hear this person's story, and you
have to give them a chance to tell it. (Many of the blockers we discuss
below are the opposite of open-ended questions.) You should think about
questions that invite people to tell their stories, including details and specific circumstances. The richer the details, the richer the conversation.

Follow-up questions
    A conversation isn't an interrogation nor the cross-examination of a
witness in court. Follow-up questions should be looking to open up space
and explain details, rather than aggressively grilling someone on what
they've said. If your relationship is strong, "Can you explain…?" is a
fine follow-up, but it certainly can sound like "You need to explain yourself because you've done/said something wrong" and misfire. You can't
go wrong with "Tell me more about…," referencing ideas, implications,
and details of what you've heard. And, of course, follow-up questions
should show that you were listening to what was already said.

Back-channeling

Back-channeling (Yule, 1996) refers to the verbal and non-verbal feedback behaviors that show, in real time, you are still listening. Back-channeling includes nodding, smiling, saying "mm-hmm," and "uh huh" (it's hard to spell how that sounds in US English, but it has a down-up intonation pattern). What back-channeling does is maintain your connection while the other person is speaking. The reason this is important is that if you stop back-channeling, the other person will assume there is something wrong and will often stop and ask what's wrong. It's especially important, when the conversation topic is difficult or sensitive, to create a positive, non-judgmental environment. This can be surprisingly hard, because we are used to giving a clear reaction to people and things we disagree with – knitted eyebrows, frowns, "C'mon!" "No way!" "Please," and so on. Practice keeping a look of pleasant interest on your face and give regular positive feedback.

Positive feedback

Conversations, even hard ones, go better when praise for the other person and their contributions are explicit. Be generous with praise. No matter how much you disagree with what the person is telling you, or even how angry it makes you, you have to remember that this person is doing you the courtesy of being willing to share it with you. That's not easy; nobody likes exposing themselves to judgment. When someone finishes a story, it's great to thank them, or even say "Wonderful!" or "Excellent!" with sincerity. Taking time out, every once in a while, to just say you appreciate the conversation and the effort will go a long way toward making a conversation productive. A similar tactic is the *check-in*. Whether you think there's a problem or not, it's good, every so often, to check in with the other person about how they feel the conversation is going. The most common response will be "Oh, fine, no problem," but that's OK, since it still shows your interest in a positive interaction. If you do it often enough, though, you may get a more nuanced response ("It's going well, but I'd still prefer you didn't refer to members of the LDS church as Mormons").

Blockers

Some things you do, intentionally or thoughtlessly, make conversations difficult, less productive, and maybe hostile. Here are some things to avoid. Remember that in some contexts they might not be terrible, but in a difficult conversation, even with someone you are close to, they can cause problems.

Hostile questions

These can include fake questions ("You don't really believe that, do you?") or tests ("So what exactly is the difference between an mRNA vaccine and a regular one?"). Hostile questions put someone on the spot, and the subtext is that a "wrong" answer would be shameful. Sometimes these are called "bear trap questions," which are designed to get you stuck regardless of the response you make.

Assertions disguised as questions

Sometimes people try to add an assertion ("This is something true") to a conversation, which is appropriate – unless the assertion is disguised as a question. Putting it in the form of the question may manipulate the other person into agreeing with it more easily than they otherwise would. Sometimes it can look like "Aren't all vaccines really dangerous?" This is asserting the danger of vaccines, which is fine, but it's not a real question and doesn't add to engagement. Earlier, we discussed factive verbs, and those come into play here. A question with a factive verb presumes its own answer. If you say "Don't you realize vaccines are dangerous?", it's unclear how to respond. If you say "yes," then you've agreed with the assertion "vaccines are dangerous," but if you say "no," then it sounds like you've made a mistake because you should know this – even if you disagree with it.

Using trigger words or hyperbole

Hyperbole, a kind of exaggeration, is hard to engage. Take words like

Nobody/everybody
Always/never
Completely/totally

Few claims or topics deserve these descriptors. In most conversations, we are talking about things which are appropriately understood in the context of "it depends." As a totalizing assertion "Everybody hates vaccines" requires your conversant to try to object and say something like "Well, it depends, some do and some don't…". Then you run the risk of getting lost in the attempt to specify the context for the original claim. If it happens over and over, it's exhausting, and someone may just give up on the conversation.

Trigger words have a similar problem. Referring to abortion rights activists as "baby killers" will always create more heat than light and indicates you don't really want to have an authentic conversation. Calling those who advocate enforcing government policies you don't like "Nazis" doesn't really help create engagement about the substantive issues.

Insults

Insulting the other person, whether obviously or indirectly, isn't likely to create a great relationship. Insults can include things from "Well, that's stupid" to the more subtle "If you look at the research on this issue you'll see…," which implies the other person didn't do their homework. It would be better to reference yourself "I've looked at this research and here's what I saw…".

Disconfirmation

Disconfirmation, in human communication, happens when you frame or respond to a message in a way that rejects the value or presence of the other person (Watzlawick, Beavin and Jackson, 1967). If you've ever known someone who does conversation as extended monologues, then you've experienced this phenomenon. Disconfirmation attacks the relationship while seeming to participate in the conversation. Sometimes it takes the form of the verbal and non-verbal contradicting each other (making a face and frowning while saying "yes"); sarcasm is almost always disconfirming.

Often disconfirmation takes the form of pointing out something about the other person that is disqualifying for full, authentic engagement. "You're just saying that because your Catholic" (or insert virtually any social or personal category) or "You just don't get it because you're a man," which says outright that the other person isn't competent to engage with. Of course, there are things men don't understand well because they lack specific life experiences, but two points here matter for civility: First, a particular man may have taken the time to learn about other perspectives and may be able to talk about them in a competent and thoughtful way. Second, there might be more engaging ways of making this point to someone. Granted, that takes time and effort, and doesn't always work, but those are the burdens of civil conversation. Disconfirmation is a kind of refusal to engage, and that's why we need to avoid it to practice radical civility.

Ventriloquizing

Ventriloquizing happens when you speak for the other person. In active listening, you might say "What I hear you saying is that you feel you have good reasons to be skeptical of vaccines" and the other person has a chance to contrast that with what they meant. A ventriloquist instead inserts their own words for the other person's "So you're saying that vaccines are dangerous and you're just wrong about that." The problem here is that the ventriloquist puts words in the other person's mouth and then argues with them – clearly not engagement, not genuine conversation. And the other person is literally treated like a dummy; they may not even get a chance to give their own view until the first person is deep into their critique.

Practice 8: Privilege Stories of Mutual Understanding and Acceptance, Not Stories with Good Guys Defeating Bad Guys

Principle – Lean into hard conversations
Process – Engage in deliberation

We all tell stories. Not in the sense of saying false things, but in the sense of using narratives to tie our ideas and experiences together. Most people try to understand the world and their lives in it through different kinds of stories. Stories also have implications: "I did something and ever after felt terrible about it" implies "you shouldn't do that either." Sharing stories, especially about yourself, is a central part of civil conversations. But not all stories are created equal, and sometimes stories can lead us astray.

Simple vs. Complex Stories

Simple stories that grapple with complex problems will not be true to those problems and imply simple answers to complex questions (Stroh, 2015). "If everybody is armed, there will be no more crime" makes for a good story, but it's not a very helpful one. There isn't any good evidence for it, and it makes a lot of dubious assumptions (every crime is preventable by shooting people, everyone is willing to shoot someone to prevent crime, etc.). The core of the story is the idea that deterrence works, and of course sometimes it does, but…it depends. Complex, nuanced stories imply complex nuanced answers; complex stories are harder and not as fun, but they get us further. This is the core of productive discussions about public matters: getting into specific cases and evidence and exploring how our ideas and values play out in dialog with others.

The Good vs. The Bad Stories

A common story plot is Good vs. Evil; there is a struggle between Good People and Bad People, and after some twists and turns, the Good People win. Of course, as kids we learn something from these stories, that it's better to be good than bad. But in adult life, the roles and the story are never so clear; most situations have dimensions of both Good and Bad, as do all people (and much of the literature is meant to explore this fact). Good vs. Bad stories (the Bad Government vs. Good individual citizens or the Good Government vs. Evil Corporations) are just too easy, and though they give a strong sense of satisfaction, they aren't productive. The real problems we all face together are more like Good vs. Good and Bad vs. Bad, which are difficult but realistic.

As society, as a political system, as an economy and culture, we face Hard Choices and Wicked Problems; most of our problems are complex enough that any solution will require trading off between Goods and settling for a certain amount of Bad. Given that, civil conversations should be strong and deep enough to engage stories with plots like these:

Wise Tradeoffs
Tough Calls
Reasonable Compromises
Unexpected Reconciliations
Learning to Live with Each Other Despite Disagreement

We should offer each other stories more like these and value them, not taking the willingness to find complex solutions as moral weakness. It's not giving up on your principles to bring them into engagement with others to find new ways of thinking and moving forward.

Practice 9: Use Careful, Full Arguments, without Creating Straw Targets

Principle – Lean into hard conversations
Process – Engage in deliberation

One of the purposes of proposing radical civility as a necessary practice of citizenship is that we want to be able to engage with people that have different views in constructive ways. We have to assume, if this is an important feature of democracy, that argument is inevitable. We've written a lot about shifting our focus away from thinking about winning and losing arguments and toward understanding our interlocutors. And at its core, radical civility asks that we treat others with care as a precondition for building relationships. But we also want to be able to express our own positions and our own beliefs in meaningful ways and at important times. We need to be able to articulate our deepest held commitments, not just listen and ask questions. There are ways to do this that increase our chances of being heard and allow us to maintain relationships even if we find ourselves in deep disagreement. In other words, if we argue with, what we're calling, careful reasoning and make "full" arguments, then we set the right tone for productive deliberation.

To do this, we need to think back to our high school writing classes – and then forget some of what we were taught there. Many students are taught that they should write a paper with a "thesis" statement. A "thesis" makes it seem as if you can show that some particular position is true and makes communication, in writing or any other media, a practice of demonstration. We ought to think about argument as more a matter of making claims than demonstrating the truth of a thesis. A claim is an invitation to a response. If we articulate our beliefs or positions to someone that we suspect holds different views, then we need to expect that they'll respond, no matter what demonstration of that position we offer. Thinking about argument as a process of making claims highlights that expectation and the inevitable back and forth that will follow. If we want to generate exaggerated and emotional responses, then we can make broad, unsupported, outrageous claims. But if we want people to hear us, then we need to make careful claims that are limited in scope and well-supported by evidence and reasons. We can also use concrete and specific claims, instead of hyperbolic ones, to increase the likelihood that we'll end up in deliberative conversations that minimize the impact of emotions and allow people to be thoughtful in their responses. We also need to plant objections and recognize opposing views when we state our own claims. This shows others that we know that argument is not just a matter of proving a thesis but is actually a process of back and forth. This means that we can't expect to rest our beliefs on some bit of evidence that we take to be true and just assume that if we show this truth to someone else, they will automatically accept it. That's not how practical argument works. We need to get ready for some back and forth and use the kinds of argumentative practice that are most likely to be successful within that back and forth. How can we do this?

Use qualifiers for whatever claim you are making
A qualifier indicates the strength of an argument. It's a way of showing that you know your claim might not be true always, forever, in every circumstance, and that can be a way of telling your conversation partner that you are humble and thoughtful about your argument. Words like presumably, some, occasionally, sometimes, in certain circumstances, probably, possibly, may, might, seldom, could, few, or doubtful are all qualifiers. Using these kinds of words is a form of careful thinking.

Seek multiple reasons and multiple kinds of evidence to support your arguments
A "full" argument is one that has more than one reason to support it and lots of evidence for those reasons. If we discover one study on why mask wearing does not work, that's simply not enough to make a full argument. Or if our only reason to avoid wearing a mask is that it makes us uncomfortable, then that is also just not enough. If we can show people that we've considered multiple forms of evidence (say, for example, data, expert testimony, examples, and stories all supporting a reason) and that we've thought through several reasons why we ought to believe what we do, then we will be offering a full argument.

Anticipate and acknowledge objections and criticisms
We can, in the course of conversation, account for the most likely critiques of our position or argument. And when we do this, we can use the "steel man" technique instead of the "straw man" technique. The "steel man" technique suggests that we should articulate a criticism of our position in the strongest way possible, highlighting the best reasons and evidence to support an opposing claim. The "straw man" is a caricature of a criticism, obviously weak and intended to perform a willingness to engage another perspective without substance.

Combine all of these practices and you'll be able to have civil conversations with anyone in your life, and you'll also be widely recognized as a good communicator, someone that's easy to talk to, and someone others can trust.

We need these kinds of people populating our social world in order to make democracy function in an effective way. Without them, the democratic systems will collapse. We can call this collapse a result of polarization, bad rules or procedures, or the backsliding of democratic norms, but whatever we call it we can be sure that these specific communication practices are likely absent if a democracy is threatening to unravel. Therefore, our best means of preserving democracy is through these practices of radical civility as the glue that will hold it all together.

5 The Payoff

Democracy is an activity, not just an abstract set of principles or governance structures. As an activity, citizens in a democracy can choose either to do democracy or to undo it. Recently, those engaged in the undoing have received a lot of attention and made remarkable advances, while those interested in the doing of democracy seem to be retreating. These trends might just reverse themselves in the next few years or they could get worse and end the entire American democratic experiment. We aren't here to offer a prediction on which course is more likely. We have offered a granular, detailed analysis of what doing democracy looks like as a matter of the most everyday common habit of citizenship we all practice: communication. By democracy, we don't (just) mean systems in which people vote and choose their leaders, but ones in which that voting is preceded by broad public deliberation, from the interpersonal to the mediated context. The approach to communication described in this book is necessary for doing participatory democracy, especially when we are talking about modern large-scale, multi-cultural democracies characterized by high degrees of diversity, like in the United States. Deeply inclusive democracy has been difficult to achieve, and neither the United States nor any other country has met the standards for it. It wasn't until just over a century ago in the United States that women were finally granted the vote!

We need to be clear that setting a high standard of inclusion creates the need for civility. A deeply inclusive democracy is one where *everyone*, in the broadest possible sense, can participate in public decision-making (can both speak and be heard), and where the system welcomes diversity, in terms of identities, values, beliefs, commitments, interests, or styles of engagement. Simpler forms of civility, like politeness or decorum, may have been necessary for democracies of white, land-owning men, but now those forms of politeness or decorum can manifest themselves as a tactic for suppressing difference and maintaining the status quo (Washington/Conway, 2019). Therefore, we need a more radical form of civility, one that can create the conditions for engaging deep differences in meaningful ways because the constructive, cooperative engagement of difference is a necessary practice in doing any form of democracy. We have been trying to radicalize civility by going to its roots as a method of engaging difference respectfully.

DOI: 10.4324/9781003442165-5

How would our world be different if we all started practicing radical civility as we've outlined it? We would certainly not be living in a blissful, peaceful, perfect fairy tale of sunshine and roses. We'd all still experience difference and disagreement, especially around values, beliefs, and recommendations for future courses of action. But we'd have a constructive approach for managing all of that difference and disagreement instead of a destructive approach that threatens to wreck the democratic systems we inhabit. This is a critical difference. Growing "affective polarization" and "negative partisan" attitudes plague our present moment (Edsall, 2023). These develop when people's social identity merges with their racial, religious, political, and sexual identity and that combination works to drive an emotional type of othering, aversion, and moral judgment about people that do not belong to our social identity. The attitudes that are generated from affective polarization threaten democratic norms and procedures because they make our fellow citizens into our enemies. They also erode trust in one another and trust in social institutions. Radical civility would prevent this kind of outcome, whereby others are enemies with whom we have nothing in common and with whom we cannot reach binding and collective decisions. In the place of affective polarization, we might find a collaborative and cooperative social fabric whereby difference is not a source of moral judgment but a resource for better decisions. The ideal of democracy is that we can leverage the insight, knowledge, and perspective of diverse peoples to make better decisions and improve outcomes in all sorts of ways. From such a perspective, difference and disagreement are a resource for constructive ends and not an inspiration for demonization. The pivot from demonization of the other to collaboration with the other is necessary for doing democracy well. For whatever reason that pivot seems especially difficult in our moment. Radical civility teaches us how to make that move in very specific, local, and practical ways. We could change our democratic systems to make them more inclusive and resilient, but systems-level change might not matter if our social fabric remains as acrimonious as it is right now. We could improve how our institutions function, but, again, doing so might not matter if distrust and disdain between citizens remain the way it is now. To radicalize civility is to get to the most fundamental root of democratic life – encounters between two people that hold different views and values but that need to find a way to live well with one another on an equal footing. A lot can be gained by changing those encounters.

What Are the Results of Practicing Radical Civility?

We are arguing that the practice of radical civility will have three major consequences. First, by repairing the social fabric, building trust between strangers, and prioritizing the maintenance of relationships in political life, we reduce the kinds of polarization that threaten democratic systems. This is a method of lowering the stakes of our disagreements so that not every decision feels like life or death, and a method for making sure we treat our fellow citizens as potential friends and not as enemies despite differences between us. The payoffs of repairing the social fabric might not be as obvious as a piece of legislation that provides health care to those that need it or a new bridge in our town that makes travel easier. But better relationships can lead to all sorts of unpredictable change. We simply cannot do the work of democracy without functional relationships. The more we treat fellow citizens as enemies or dangerous others, the more we threaten the basic conditions for doing democracy. We must find ways to move past these forms of demonizing fellow citizens, and radicalizing civility is one means for doing so. Weaving together the social fabric is a critical way to rebuild the trust in social institutions that seems missing now.

Second, these kinds of communication practices open up spaces for changes to beliefs, behaviors, and commitments. By prioritizing relationships over the making and defending of arguments, we do more to diffuse reactance or defensiveness and instead create an environment whereby people feel safe to engage in careful deliberation, weigh different perspectives, and decide to make changes. In other words, strong, constructive, and trusting relationships are often necessary ingredients for changing people's positions, and the practices of radical civility are the means toward such ends. This approach to politics opens the space for change instead of forcing change on others that are resisting and will grow resentful after losing a "political battle." We cannot predict when change will happen or what magic words will alter someone's perspective. Also, we do know that change only happens in the presence of functional, trusting, constructive relationships.

Third, radical civility is the path to the deepest forms of inclusion. The goal of any democratic system or way of life should be to broadly incorporate as many citizens as possible in decision-making procedures. But if we see difference as a source of animosity and resentment, then people will either intentionally distance themselves from politics (because they feel unwelcome, unrecognized, and unappreciated), or people will be excluded by practices of demonization that ostracize some groups from public life (sometimes by rules or laws and other times by social mores or habits). But radical civility encourages the broadest possible forms of participation by seeking out a way to understand and respect differences. Prioritizing relationship building and maintenance is the best way to prioritize inclusivity.

The Hardest Cases Can Still Produce Change

We have no shortage of difficult cases in our moment – politicians rolling back basic voting rights and trying to steal elections, white supremacists glorifying Nazis and threatening a race war, religious restrictions over women's bodies, and many other extreme views that seem to creep ever further into the mainstream of political discourse. We have also probably seen difficult cases in our own everyday lives – our neighbor shouting at us because we parked our car in front of their house, a high school friend trolling us on Facebook or Twitter, a local business place refusing to serve people who have received the COVID-19 vaccine. These examples provide the deepest challenge to radical civility. We do not want to engage some of these extreme characters. We fear that respectful engagement with toxic, extreme, and hateful views is a mistake and that no good will come from engagement with views that we find noxious. But we have good reasons, moral and practical, to choose civility even in the face of bad faith opposition. Civility can work, as a communication practice, to alter, or redirect, conversations to more constructive paths. Civility is also a moral good in a democracy and allows us to foster change and not force it.

Change is not a simple equation or a clear and direct path. We hope for change and we try to create the conditions in which change happens. This remains true even in these difficult and extreme cases. Persuasion is not a light switch that we can easily flick on or off. It is a slow, difficult process, and the most challenging cases require the most concentrated, long-lasting, and disciplined work. To focus on relationships over strategically advancing specific political positions is to take a risk, especially when we're engaged with the most difficult and extreme cases. That risk requires a belief that building a durable, trusting relationship can make anything possible. It's hard work, the kind of work that can feel hopeless or un-acknowledged, but it's the work of democracy. To give up on the hardest cases is to refuse to do democracy when it matters the most. And the imperfect, uneven results of attending to these hard cases are emblematic of democracy as a way of life in general. We don't know where it might lead and what changes might await us, but we do know that constructive engagement is the only non-violent path available to us.

We Can Save the Democratic Experiment by Rebuilding the Social Fabric

Democracy is under threat right now; that much seems clear. Those of us that wish to defend participatory democracy, because of the values of freedom and equality that it prioritizes, need both arguments for why we ought to save it and recommendations for how to save it. We're not suggesting that radical civility is all that we need to reverse the rising tides of fascism and authoritarianism that we are seeing across the world. But we are suggesting that this is a necessary, fundamental component of any attempt to breathe new life into democracies across the world. When citizens believe that relationships matter and that difference is not a personal affront but an imaginative resource, then democracy can flourish and provide the advantages of prosperity, innovation, and peace that we've seen it provide in other times and places. If democracy is a way of life before it is a system of government, then rehabilitating that way of life requires a commitment to some form of radical civility.

Constitutions, systems of governance, rules and regulations are not enough to make real and vibrant the values of equality and freedom. We need everyday practices of communication to live inside those structures and to make the promise of democracy real for as many citizens as possible. Repairing the social fabric in order for people to see that we are all interconnected and dependent on one another in meaningful ways is the best way to make sure that the structures of democracy survive and thrive. To radicalize civility is to turn toward the project of relationship making and maintenance that can save the democratic experiment. That's a lofty claim – communicate in the ways prescribed in this book and you'll have transformative, unexpected relationships. These relationships are the soil within which the structures of democracy must grow; without them it's hard to see how democracy might bear fruit.

References

Acho, Emmanuel. 2020. *Uncomfortable Conversations with a Black Man*. New York: Flatiron Books.

Alinsky, Saul. 1989. *Rules for Radicals: A Pragmatic Primer on Realistic Radicals*. New York: Vintage Press.

Aronson, Eliot. 1999. "The Power of Self-Persuasion." *The American Psychologist* 5411: 875–884. https://doi.org/10.1037/h0088188.

Beaufort, Maren, ed. 2020. *Digital Media, Political Polarization, and the Challenge to Democracy*. New York: Routledge Press.

Bishop, Bill. 2009. *The Big Sort: Why the Clustering of Like-Minded Americans is Tearing us Apart*. New York: Houghton Mifflin Harcourt.

Boatright, Robert G., Timothy J. Shaffer, Sarah Sobieraj, and Dannagal Goldthwaite Young, eds. 2019. *A Crisis of Civility? Political Discourse and Its Discontents*. New York: Routledge.

Bohm, David. 2013. *On Dialogue*. London: Routledge.

Bowden, Michelle. 2022. *How to Persuade: The Skills You Need to Get What You Want*. Hoboken: Wiley Press.

Brehm, Sharon, and Jack Brehm. 1991. *Psychological Reactance: A Theory of Freedom and Control*. New York: Brace Jovanovich.

Buber, Martin. 1971. *I and Thou*. New York: Free Press.

Carey, James. 1992. *Communication as Culture: Essays on Media and Society*. New York: Routledge Press.

Carse, James. 1987. *Finite and Infinite Games*. New York: Ballantine Books.

Catmull, Ed, and Amy Wallace. 2014. *Creativity, Inc.: Overcoming the Unseen Forces That Stand in the Way of True Inspiration*. New York: Random House.

Chenoweth, Erica, and Maria Stephan. 2012. *Why Civil Resistance Works: The Strategic Logic of Nonviolent Conflict*. New York: Columbia University Press.

Christakis, Nicholas, and James Fowler. 2011. *Connected: The Surprising Power of Our Social Networks and How They Shape Our Lives – How Your Friends' Friends' Friends Affect Everything You Feel, Think, and Do*. New York: Little, Brown Spark.

Cialdini, Robert. 2006. *Influence: The Psychology of Persuasion*. New York: Harper Business.

Cialdini, Robert. 2018. *Pre-Suasion: A Revolutionary Way to Influence and Persuade*. New York: Simon & Schuster.

Clark, Dan. 2022. *Story Selling: How to Persuade People to Think, Feel, Act, Follow, Buy*. Dallas: Izzard Inc. Publishing.

Coleman, Peter. 2021. *The Way Out: How to Overcome Toxic Polarization*. New York: Columbia University Press.

Conway, Moncure, and George Washington. 2019. *George Washington's Rules of Civility*. Digireads.com.

Csikszentmihalyi, Mihaly. 2008. *Flow: The Psychology of Optimal Experience*. New York: Harper Perennial Modern Classics.

Danisch, Robert. 2012. "The Roots and Form of Obama's Rhetorical Pragmatism." *Rhetoric Review* 31: 148–168.

Dewey, John. 2016. *The Public and Its Problems: An Essay in Political Inquiry*. Chicago: Swallow Press.

Edsall, Thomas. 2023. "Meet the People Working on Getting Us to Hate One Another Less." *The New York Times*, February 8, 2023.

Fisher, Max. 2022. *The Chaos Machine: The Inside Story of How Social Media Rewired Our Minds and Our World*. New York: Little, Brown and Company.

Forni, Pietro M. 2003. *Choosing Civility: Twenty-Five Rules of Considerate Conduct*. New York: St. Martin's Griffin.

Ganz, Marshall. 2009. *Why David Sometimes Wins: Leadership, Organization, and Strategy in the California Farm Worker Movement*. New York: Oxford University Press.

Gibb, Jack. 1961. "Defensive Communication." *Journal of Communication* 11 (3): 141–148. https://doi.org/10.1111/j.1460-2466.1961.tb00344.x.

Goldstein, N., S. Martin, and Robert Cialdini. 2009. *Yes!: 50 Scientifically Proven Ways to Be Persuasive*. New York: Free Press.

Gottman, John. 1995. *Why Marriages succeed or Fail: And How You Can Make Yours Last*. New York: Simon & Schuster.

Granovetter, Mark. 1973. "The Strength of Weak Ties." *American Journal of Sociology* 78 (6): 1360–1380.

Guzman, Monica. 2022. *I Never Thought of it That Way: How to Have Fearlessly Curious Conversations in Dangerously Divided Times*. Dallas: BenBella Books.

Hari, Johann. 2022. *Stolen Focus: Why You Can't Pay Attention – And How to Think Deeply Again*. New York: Crown Publishing.

Hartman, Andrew. 2019. *A War for the Soul of America: A History of the Culture Wars*. Chicago: University of Chicago Press.

Hauser, Gerard. 2002. *Introduction to Rhetorical Theory*. Boston: Waveland Press.

Hayward, Bob. 2018. *Persuade: How to Persuade Anyone About Anything*. London: Panoma Press.

Kahneman, Daniel. 2013. *Thinking Fast and Slow*. New York: Anchor Press.

Klein, Ezra. 2021. *Why We are Polarized*. New York: Simon & Schuster.

Kommers, Cody. 2018. "Why Republicans Listen to Country Music and Democrats Don't." *Psychology Today*. https://www.psychologytoday.com/us/blog/friendly-interest/201809/why-republicans-listen-country-music-and-democrats-don-t.

Lakoff, George. 2016. *Moral Politics: How Liberals and Conservatives Think*. Chicago: University of Chicago Press.

Levitsky, Steve, and Daniel Ziblatt. 2019. *How Democracies Die*. New York: Crown Press.

Lieberman, Matthew. 2014. *Social: Why Our Brains Are Wired to Connect*. New York: Crown Press.

Mason, Liliana. 2018. *Uncivil Agreement: How Politics Became Our Identity*. Chicago: University of Chicago Press.

Matthews, David. 2014. *The Ecology of Democracy: Finding Ways to Have a Stronger hand in Shaping Our Future*. Dayton: Kettering Foundation Press.

McCarty, Nolan. 2019. *Polarization: What Everyone Needs to Know*. New York: Oxford University Press.

Metts, Sandra, and William Cupach. 2008. "Face Theory: Goffman's Dramatistic Approach to Interpersonal Interaction." In *Engaging Theories in Interpersonal Communication: Multiple Perspectives*, edited by Dawn O. Braithewaite and Paul Schrodt, 229–240. Los Angeles: Sage Publishing.

Miller, Tim. 2022. *Why We Did It: A Travelogue from the Republican Road to Hell*. New York: Harper.

Miller, William, and Stephen Rollnick. 2012. *Motivational Interviewing: Helping People Change*. New York: The Guilford Press.

Mixon, Harold, and Mary Francis Hopkins. 1989. "Apocalypticism in Secular Public Discourse: A Proposed Theory." *Central States Speech Journal* 39: 244–257.

Mounk, Yascha. 2022. https://www.theatlantic.com/ideas/archive/2022/05/us-democrat-republican-partisan-polarization/629925.

Mull, Amanda. 2019. "America Blew It on Arugala." *The Atlantic Monthly*. https://www.theatlantic.com/health/archive/2019/03/arugula-rocks-come-at-me-spinach/585571/.

Neufeld, Blain. 2022. *Public Reason and Political Autonomy: Realizing the Ideal of a Civic People*. New York: Routledge.

Nichols, John, and Robert McChesney. 2006. *Tragedy and Farce: How the American Media Sell Wars, Spin Elections, and Destroy Democracy*. New York: The New Press.

Oakes, Penelope, and Alexander Haslam. 1994. *Stereotyping and Social Reality*. Hoboken: Wiley-Blackwell.

Pentland, Alex. 2015. *Social Physics: How Social Networks Can Make Us Smarter*. New York: Penguin Books.

Peters, John Durham. 2001. *Speaking Into the Air: A History of the Idea of Communication*. Chicago: University of Chicago Press.

Recovery Village. 2022. "The Rise in Gambling Addition." https://www.therecoveryvillage.com/process-addiction/compulsive-gambling/rise-in-video-gambling-addiction/.

Reddy, Michael. 1993. "The Conduit Metaphor – A Case of Frame Conflict in Our Language about Language." In *Metaphor and Thought*, edited by Andrew Ortony, 2nd ed., 164–201. Cambridge: Cambridge University Press.

Redmond, Timothy. 2022. *Political Tribalism in America: How Hyper-Partisanship Dumbs Down Democracy and How to Fix It*. Jefferson: McFarland and Company, Inc.

Renkl, Margaret. 2018. "How to Talk to a Racist: White Liberals, You're Doing It All Wrong." *New York Times*. https://www.nytimes.com/2018/07/30/opinion/how-to-talk-to-a-racist.html.

Rosenfeld, Sam. 2017. *The Polarizers: Postwar Architects of Our Partisan Era*. Chicago: University of Chicago Press.

Schein, Edgar. 2013. *Humble Inquiry: The Gentle Art of Asking Instead of Telling*. Oakland: Berrett-Koehler Publishers.

Schneirov, Richard, and Gaston Fernandez. 2013. *Democracy as a Way of Life in America: A History*. New York: Routledge Press.

Shirky, Clay. 2008. *Here Comes Everybody: How Change Happens When People Come Together*. New York: Penguin Group.

Smith, Eleanor. 2019. *Stop Being Reasonable: How We Really Change Our Minds*. New York: Public Affairs Books.

Stroh, David Peter. 2015. "Deciphering the Plots of Systems Stories." In *Systems Thinking for Social Change: A Practical Guide to Solving Complex Problems, Avoiding Unintended Consequences, and Achieving Lasting Results*, 45–70. New York: Chelsea Green Publishing.

Talbot, Margaret. 2021. "The Increasingly Wild World of School Board Meetings." *The New Yorker*. https://www.newyorker.com/news/daily-comment/the-increasingly -wild-world-of-school-board-meetings.

Taplin, Jonathan. 2017. *Move Fast and Break Things: How Facebook, Google, and Amazon Cornered Culture and Undermined Democracy*. New York: Little, Brown and Company.

Tardy, Charles and Joy Smithson. 2018. "Self-Disclosure: Strategic Revelation of Information in Personal and Professional Relationships." In *The Handbook of Communication Skills*, edited by Owen Hargie, 217–258. New York: Routledge.

The Waycroft. 22 July, 2020. "The Loudest Neighbors in the US: A Survey." https:// thewaycroft.com/noisy-neighbors/.

"Tittha Sutta: Sectarians 1" Ud 6.4, translated from the Pali by Thanissaro Bhikkhu. 2012. *Access to Insight BCBS Edition*. http://www.accesstoinsight.org/tipitaka/kn /ud/ud.6.04.than.html.

Turkle, Sherry. 2017. *Alone Together: Why We Expect More From Technology and Less From Each Other*. New York: Basic Books.

Vaidhyanathan, Siva. 2021. *Antisocial Media: How Facebook Disconnects Us and Undermines Democracy*. New York: Oxford University Press.

Watzlawick, Paul, Janet Beavin, and Don Jackson. 1967. *The Pragmatics of Human Communication*. New York: W.W. Norton.

Waldinger, Robert, and Marc Schulz. 2023. *The Good Life: Lessons from the World's Longest Scientific Study of Happiness*. New York: Simon & Schuster.

Weinberger, David. 2008. *Small Pieces Loosely Joined: A Unified Theory of the Web*. New York: Basic Books.

Williams, James. 2020. *How to Make People Do What You Want: Methods of Subtle Psychology to Read People, Persuade, and Influence Human Behavior*. Independently Published.

Wittgenstein, Ludwig. 2010. *Philosophical Investigations*. Hoboken: Wiley-Blackwell.

Yule, George. 1996. *Pragmatics*. New York: Oxford University Press.

Zamalin, Alex. 2021. *Against Civility: The Hidden Racism in Our Obsession with Civility*. Boston: Beacon Press.

Index